The Complete Book of the

DOG

The Complete Book of the

DOG

SARAH WHITEHEAD

CHANCELLOR
PRESS

Photography by Jane Burton, Paddy Cutts & Marc Henri

First published in 1999
under the title THE COMPLETE BOOK OF THE DOG
By Chancellor Press, an imprint of Bounty Books, a division of Octopus Publishing Group Ltd.
2–4 Heron Quays, Docklands, London, E14 4JP

This is a Prima Editions Book
Orleton Road, Ludlow Business Park, Ludlow, Shropshire SY8 1XF, England

For Prima Editions
Editorial Director: Roger Kean
Creative Director: Oliver Frey
Series Editor: Iain MacGregor
Copy Editor: Neil Williams
Design: Joanne Dovey, Charlotte Kirby
Four-Color Separation: Prima Creative Services, England

Printed and bound in Italy by Rotolito Lombarda

ISBN: 0-7537-0141-3

the origin of
dogs

above: *The fox is regarded as a cousin of the domestic dog.*

left: *The noble wolf.*

Man and dog have been associated for thousands of years. However, long before this, the dog's wild ancestors lived without human contact, populating many areas of the world in many different habitats.

the **dog** family

There is now little doubt that the domestic dog is directly descended from the wolf. However, looking at the whole dog family gives us clues about why some of their most distinctive physical and behavioral characteristics arose through evolution and the survival of the fittest.

Scientific advances in genetics mean that we can now tell exactly how closely related different species really are. Deoxyribonucleic acid, or DNA, is the molecule of heredity. A chromosome is a long strand of DNA coiled on itself that contains genes that carry specific information. This genetic information is like a fingerprint—it makes the animal absolutely unique, and also contains

elements that ensure that it resembles its parents and other members of the same family or species.

The domestic dog *(Canis familiaris)* has 78 chromosomes: 38 pairs, plus X and Y, like the wolf *(Canis lupus)*, the coyote *(Canis latrans)*, and the jackal *(Canis aureus)*. Only animals with the same number of chromosomes can breed together successfully, which means these three animals are closely related in genetic terms.

the wolf *Canis lupus*
Wolves can be large or relatively small. They vary greatly in color and

above: *A Black Backed Jackal on the alert. Jackals tend to live in pairs or small groups, unlike the wolf,* **left**, *which is a pack animal.*

coat length, as an adaptation to their environment. For example, the white coat of the Arctic Wolf helps to conceal it in ice and snow, while the grays, browns, and blacks of wolves that live in more temperate regions help them to remain hidden in grass and vegetation.

Reserved and aloof, yet living in a social structure that in many ways reflects our own family unit, the wolf has become almost legendary for its behavior and beauty. Simultaneously loved and feared worldwide, it commands awe and respect, yet has been hunted and rendered almost extinct in some areas.

The number of wolves living a wild existence has now been reduced to the point where several of the probable 38 variations, including the Japanese Wolf, the Kenai Wolf, and the Newfoundland White Wolf, are now extinct. Many others in the same species face extinction, too, as their habitats are destroyed by farming and their predatory nature makes them targets for local people.

Wolves are pack animals, and although the size of the pack varies according to the resources available, the pack structure or "hierarchy" is usually stable. An "Alpha" pair have overall control of the rest of the pack, deciding when they hunt, move den sites, and eat. The top dog and bitch are usually the only ones to breed, but the young are raised by many "aunts" and "uncles" who provide food and protection.

Physical conflicts between pack members are rare, as communication systems are so effective. Wolves use facial expression, body language, vocalizations, and olfactory communication to signal to each other, making them an effective team, able to bring down much larger prey than if they hunted solo.

the coyote *Canis latrans*

The coyote is famous for its howl. Although its communication systems are not as complex as those of the wolf, coyotes live in small family groups in many parts of the world— often taking advantage of areas where the wolf has become extinct.

the jackal *Canis aureus*

Jackals live in small groups or pairs, depending on the sub-species and the amount of food available. Jackals have successfully adapted to living in many different areas. The Simien, Silverbacked, and Sidestriped jackals all live in Africa. *Canis aureus*, the Golden Jackal, is found as far east as Burma.

More distant and diverse relatives of the dog family are included in other genera. Foxes, African Wild Dogs, Dholes, Maned Wolves, Bush Dogs, and several other fox-like animals are related to the dog, although they look and behave quite differently.

above: *Once regarded as pests, dingoes live as feral dogs in their native Australia. Only a few are kept as pets.*

below: *Smaller and less sociable, the fox shares many dog-like adaptive qualities.*

domestication

The enduring relationship between man and dog is truly ancient. Early cave paintings show man and dog hunting together, and bones excavated in archeological explorations show that dogs have lived alongside man for at least 14,000 years.

Theories about how this relationship originally formed abound. The most commonly held belief is that wolves began to hang around human encampments, feeding off waste and leftovers. In return for this free supply of food, wolves acted as an early-warning system—alerting man to the presence of dangerous animals and even going on hunts in order to share the kill. Perhaps some children found a wolf cub and decided to keep it as their own—hand-rearing the animal to ensure that it was tame and treating it as the first ever "pet."

However, more recent studies have begun to question this view of the beginning of the human/canine relationship. Wolves are truly wild animals. They are expert predators and

hunters, and appear to be "pre-wired" as such. Indeed, even where wolves have been hand-reared from birth, brought up entirely as domestic pets, they eventually develop into fully grown predators and would revert to a natural hunting lifestyle if given the opportunity.

Such findings have led scientists to explore the possibility that the dog's history is somewhat more complicated, yet still inextricably connected with mankind's. There is little doubt that at the time the human lifestyle was changing from nomadic hunter to

left: Social creatures through and through, wolves depend on each other for survival and companionship.

above: The relationship between man and dog has traditionally been based on a working partnership.

settler, wolves would have congregated around dumping sites on the edge of villages. The waste around settlements would have been a good source of scavengable food, and those wolves that were less fearful of man would have come closer and gotten more to eat. In return, people would probably have placed wolves on their own menu.

Some of the "brave" cubs might have been brought inside the encampments to be "fattened up" and used as an easily obtainable food source, while others that showed skill at chasing away wild animals or alerting people to

danger might have escaped the cooking pot and become watchdogs. At this point it was likely that some sort of genetic shift took place. Man had selectively kept and bred from less reactive wolves with juvenile behaviors, and this is what remained in the genetic makeup.

To become an effective part of a hunting team, an adult wolf needs to develop a full sequence of predatory behaviors. "Eye" is required—to spot and recognize prey. "Stalk" is needed to be able to get close enough to the prey without detection. "Chase" is required to run the animal down, followed by "Bite," in order to hold it while other members of the pack arrive, and finally, "Kill." This is known as the "Eye-Stalk-Chase-Bite-Kill" sequence of an adult predator.

Inevitably, some of these early domesticated dogs would have been better at hunting than others. With their development arrested at different points, some dogs would have been ideal for stalking, without going on to kill. These would make ideal herding dogs. Equally, some would have remained extremely adolescent and playful, without any

vestige of dominant or predatory traits, and they would have been ideal for guarding livestock. Others might have had a pronounced possessive instinct over objects, and these would probably have been encouraged if there was a need for a retriever on the hunt.

In this way, those dogs that were good at tasks that man found useful were kept and bred from, while the others would have been killed and eaten. Man did not care what these dogs looked like, only what the

above: *No matter how far from its ancestral roots, the drive to act on pre-wired urges is strong.*

animal did. These permanently neotenized, juvenile wolves were playful, exuberant, and content to follow the leadership of others. Their descendants were to become our domesticated dogs.

below: *Expert hunters, all members of the dog family show superb hunting abilities and the drive to catch prey in all kinds of conditions.*

A dog is a finely tuned hunting machine. Although our domestic pets rarely have the opportunity to show off this prowess in a natural way, just watching a dog chasing after a ball or jumping over a fallen tree is enough to remind us of their athleticism, speed, and grace.

the natural
dog

above: *A coyote in full voice, a symbol of the natural world.*

left: *Working as a team—dogs have retained this natural drive.*

the basic dog

Dogs are one of the most adaptable creatures on earth. They are found thriving in temperatures ranging from well below zero to hot desert climates. As a social species they have the ability to communicate, to hunt as a team, and to settle disputes without bloodshed. With such a range of abilities, perhaps it's no wonder that humans took dogs into their homes—and into their hearts.

A dog's body system is geared toward survival and development. As a fellow mammal, many of their internal organs correspond to our own, and perform similar functions.

breathing

In order for dogs to achieve high speeds and endurance on the hunt, the lungs have developed to fill almost the

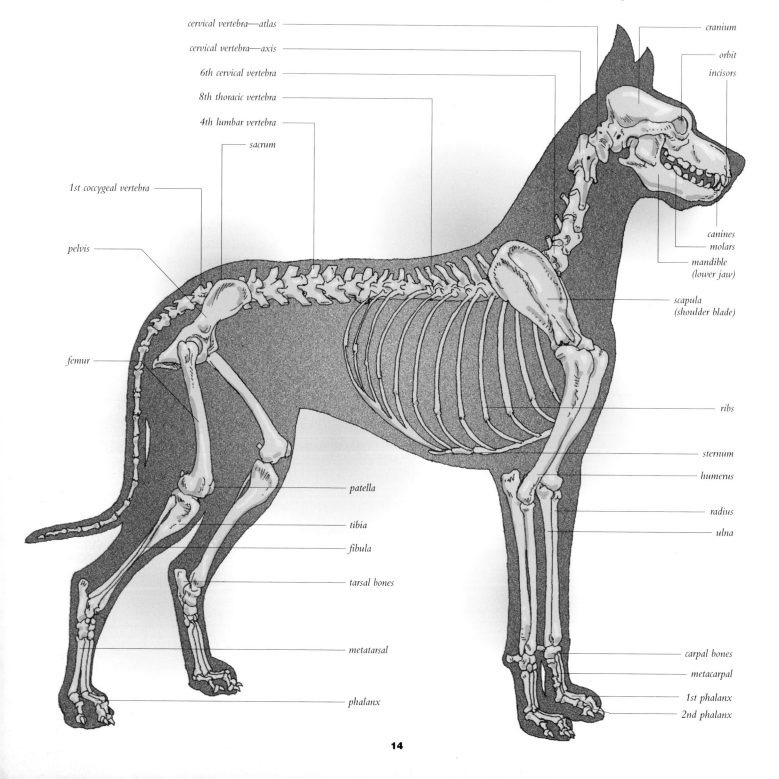

cervical vertebra—atlas
cervical vertebra—axis
6th cervical vertebra
8th thoracic vertebra
4th lumbar vertebra
sacrum
1st coccygeal vertebra
pelvis
femur
patella
tibia
fibula
tarsal bones
metatarsal
phalanx

cranium
orbit
incisors
canines
molars
mandible (lower jaw)
scapula (shoulder blade)
ribs
sternum
humerus
radius
ulna
carpal bones
metacarpal
1st phalanx
2nd phalanx

entire thoracic cavity not taken up by the heart. Oxygen is taken in and carbon dioxide removed, just as in the human system. At rest, most dogs breathe at around 10–30 times per minute, although this can rapidly accelerate during hard exercise.

eating

The dog's mouth, teeth, and digestive tract are quite different from our own. As a true omnivore, dogs are designed to eat anything and everything, including some vegetable matter—but have a carnivore's teeth for killing and tearing meat. Food is taken into the mouth and is passed down over the larynx, into the esophagus. This is a wide canal compared to that of a human and means that dogs are able to swallow relatively large lumps of food—or inappropriate objects, such as tennis balls or stones.

Once nutrients have been extracted by the digestive tract, waste products are filtered from the system through the kidneys and bowel.

reproduction

In the male dog, sperm is produced in the testicles, which lie within a protective sac, called the scrotum, outside the body. The testicles descend to this position relatively early in male puppies—anytime between eight and 20 weeks old. In some cases only a single testicle descends—a condition called *unilateral cryptorchidism*, while in

others, neither descend. Either of these conditions may require surgery in the domestic dog, as retained testicles can become malignant.

In the female, sexual maturity is reached anywhere between six and 15 months, when she has her first season. Eggs are produced in the ovaries, and then move through the fallopian tubes to the uterus. The uterus in a bitch is a very distinct shape, having two "horns" that meet at the cervix. During pregnancy, the fetuses are positioned like peas in a pod in rows along each horn.

the nervous system and brain

The dog's central nervous system consists of the brain and spinal cord. The spinal cord extends from the brain, all the way down the center of the vertebral column, to the base of

the tail. Nerve receptors gather information about the environment and the dog's position, and feed it back to the spinal cord and brain.

Very little is known about the functioning of the dog's brain. There can be no doubt that dogs have learning centers and areas that deal with sensory information—particularly the sense of smell and vision. Because dogs also have areas of the brain that correspond to those in our own that deal with emotions and memory, it seems logical that they too can experience what we describe as moods and feelings.

Dogs have survived, evolved, and flourished in many of the most difficult and extreme conditions in the world. Clearly, their physical adaptability has made this possible—but their ability to learn, communicate, and adopt social contact with another species has been their greatest asset, which is dealt with in detail in the next chapter.

the sensitive dog

A dog can see, hear, smell, and taste in much the same way a human can, but in comparison with us, dogs have heightened abilities in the first three functions.

sight

As one of the most adaptable hunting machines ever built, the dog has developed specifically in order to catch and kill prey. However, long before they can do this, dogs need to be able to find their prey, and visual sensitivity is one of the primary methods they have evolved to achieve this.

The dog's eye is relatively flat in comparison to a human's. The canine eye is designed to allow the shape of the lens to change in order to alter the focal length, but this is not as flexible as a human eye.

Compared to human vision, dogs' eyes are more sensitive to light and movement, but they tend to be less effective at determining the outline of objects. Most owners can attest to this, as even the tiniest movement in the grass can alert a dog to the presence of a small insect or rodent, while a person standing perfectly still next to a tree or bushes in the park can be completely overlooked.

how the eye works

The eye is a fluid-filled globe, held in the eye socket in the skull by strong muscles. These muscles allow the eye to rotate up, down, and from side to side, increasing the field of vision. The outer layer of the eye is covered in a tough membrane called the sclera. The front of the eye has a transparent layer, called the cornea.

The lens is attached to the cilary body, a muscle that can contract to alter the shape of the lens so that the focal length can be altered.

The back of the eye is lined with the retina. Nerves in this area are sensitive to light and transmit messages through the optic nerve to the brain, where they are "translated" into an image. A separate area at the back of the eye, called the tapetum, is specifically designed to reflect light and maximize the dog's vision when light is poor. The presence of the tapetum creates the characteristic reflection in a dog's eyes when it is caught in a direct beam of light.

Dogs can see certain colors, primarily reds. Otherwise, they are thought to see the world in tones of gray, rather than full color. However, dogs seem able to discriminate between even subtle differences in shade and contrast, so their vision is likely to have more depth than simple black and white.

Dogs do produce tears—although not when they are unhappy, like humans do. A dog's tears are produced by the lacrimal gland, in order to keep the cornea clean and moist. Excess tears are usually carried away in small ducts situated in the inner corner of the eye. If these ducts become blocked, tears may run down the animal's face. This can cause a characteristic "red" stain on the animal's hair under the eye.

Unlike humans, dogs have a third eyelid that lies hidden in the corner of each eye. This is rarely seen, unless the animal is ill or is in very poor condition. The third eyelid serves to protect the eye by drawing horizontally across its surface.

hearing

Just rustle a bag of chips and you will know how sensitive your dog's hearing is. This is a useful adaptation in the wild, as good hearing serves a number of different functions: detecting prey; providing early warning of intruders; and allowing pack members to communicate with each other through auditory signals, sometimes over long distances.

Although the quality and range of a dog's hearing changes with age, a young, healthy dog is able to detect a sound in six hundredths of a second and, by using the muscles in the outer ear to help funnel sound into the inner

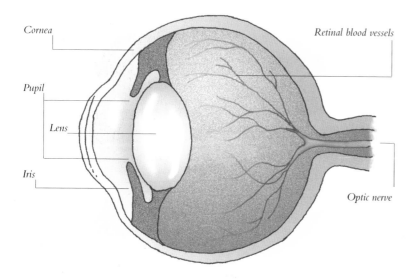

Cornea

Pupil

Lens

Iris

Retinal blood vessels

Optic nerve

left: *The ears are responsible for providing both hearing and balance. The ear canals are long and can be prone to foreign bodies—such as grass seeds— causing infection.*

The sensitivity of a dog's hearing can mean that some high-pitched sounds or very loud noises affect their ears. Training should therefore be done calmly and quietly, with soft commands, rather than shouting. The use of ultrasonic devices in training can also be detrimental—and even fuels aggression in some cases.

ear, can hear noises four times farther away than a human can. Interestingly, dogs can also shut off the inner ear to filter out background noise, in order to concentrate on a specific sound—so selective deafness in dogs is not simply a trainer's fallacy.

how the ear works

The ear is made up of four parts: the ear flap, the external ear canal, the middle ear, and the inner ear.

The size and shape of the ear flap varies considerably between breeds and types of dog. The flap protects the inner ear by covering it, and also helps to funnel the sound like a radar system through the ear canal to the ear drum.

Beyond the ear drum is the middle ear. It consists of a chamber that contains three small bones that connect the ear drum to a window at the opposite side. These bones transmit vibrations to the inner ear. Inside the inner ear, the cochlea converts these vibrations into signals that are then sent to the brain.

In the inner ear there are also organs that relate to the dog's sense of balance. These give the dog feedback about the alignment of its head in relation to the ground.

deafness

Sadly, a number of breeds now suffer from congenital deafness. This is often linked to coat color, particularly white, and can be difficult to test for without medical intervention. Deaf puppies often appear to be perfectly normal within the litter, as they follow the example of other puppies and compensate for their lack of hearing with visual awareness. Dalmatians, Bull Terriers, and white Boxers seem particularly prone to the incidence of this hereditary anomaly in either one or both ears.

Although it was once customary to cull such puppies, it has been shown that a good quality of life and a high standard of training can be achieved by those who are prepared to put in the time and effort. Deaf dogs can quickly learn to follow hand signals instead of voice commands in training, and can make good pets, given adequate time and motivation to learn. Veterinary testing for deafness in some breeds is now becoming routine and even very young pups can have their hearing accurately measured.

below: *Ear flaps can suffer from sunburn in the summer months, and frostbite in winter.*

above: *Scent chemicals in the nose send the relevant messages to the brain, which then triggers—through the limbic nerve—outward expressions of emotion.*

smell

Almost all dogs seem to spend a good part of their lives gleaning information through their noses—usually by sticking them in places where they aren't wanted! However, this ability has been well harnessed by man for centuries and makes dogs perfect for detecting drugs, illegally imported fruit, and even some cancers.

A dog's sense of smell is one inherent ability that far outstrips ours. Indeed, it is thought that it is at least one million times more acute. One reason for this is that dogs communicate via olfactory information—they can "read" scent messages left by other dogs and even prey, and respond appropriately.

how the nose works

Just like us, a dog possesses a sensitive olfactory membrane inside the nose. Molecules in the air are dissolved by the moisture on the dog's nose and inside its mouth, then captured by the surface of the membrane. Information is conveyed by nerve impulses to the olfactory center in the brain, which is large in comparison to ours.

right: *The health of the nose is maintained by flushing with a natural bacteria-killing discharge. If this system breaks down, then infection can ensue.*

Although puppies are born blind and deaf, their sense of smell is already highly developed. Just looking at a newborn puppy gives this away, as the pup's nose is large in comparison to the rest of its head and body.

The dog's sense of smell and taste are inextricably linked. Unlike us, the dog has a special organ in the roof of its mouth that can "taste" special smells. This is called the vomeronasal organ and is used primarily for scents concerned with sex. Information from this organ goes directly to the limbic system—the part of the brain connected with emotional responses. Dogs can sometimes be seen using this organ specifically if they find a really exciting smell. Typically, their teeth chatter slightly and they may drool or salivate while they taste and smell the odor at the same time.

taste

There is currently no way of identifying exactly how dogs utilize their sense of taste. While they do seem to have many of the same taste receptors as humans, the range is not so complex. This may mean that they can detect bitter, sweet, sour, and salty tastes, but perhaps not the subtleties of a four-course meal.

Some dogs seem able and willing to eat anything and everything—and enjoy even the most unusual flavors, such as raw garlic or onions. Others seem unwilling to try anything new, and will ignore anything except a familiar food. This difference may be accounted for by the effects of "food socialization"— whether or not they had the chance to

above: *Dogs are opportunist feeders, usually consuming a meal in one rapid sitting.*

experiment with different tastes and textures while young. Otherwise, it may be a case of the dog playing mind games with its owner.

how taste works

Dogs have about one-sixth of the number of taste buds that we do on our tongues, and these are mostly clustered around the anterior portion. Molecules of food land on the tongue and information about them is sent to the brain for processing, along with the smell.

Dogs sometimes make instant associations with the taste of specific foods. A dog that is sick after eating one type of food may avoid it afterward for a long period of time. This is called "taste aversion" and is a basic survival strategy to keep dogs from eating foods that would make them sick on a continual basis.

touch

For the first two weeks of their lives, puppies rely almost entirely on their senses of touch and smell. In order to survive, pups must glean body warmth from their mother and litter mates, and must learn how and where to suckle. This is activated by the "rooting

reflex," whereby the puppy moves its head from side to side to locate its mother or siblings by touch, then homes in on the nipples through smell.

The close contact that a puppy's mother provides in these early weeks establishes an enjoyment of physical contact for life. Indeed, providing that no bad experiences follow, dogs then learn to accept and enjoy physical contact in many forms, both from other dogs and humans.

The skin is the dog's main touch receptor, although the nose is also very sensitive to touch. The hair and nails themselves are much like ours, in that they are effectively "dead" and can be cut without pain, although pressure on them can still relay information back to the touch receptors.

Touch sensitivity varies greatly and tends to depend on breed characteristics and individuality. Breeds such as Bull Terriers, Staffordshire Bull Terriers, and Boxers are all regarded as relatively insensitive to touch. This is because they were bred for fighting or baiting—thus their stamina or endurance in the pit was determined by how much pain they could withstand. Other breeds, such as Shetland Sheepdogs or Collies, tend to be much more touch-sensitive, and can flinch or resist even the gentlest petting.

Feet, mouths, and tails tend to be the most sensitive areas for dogs who don't like being handled. This is perhaps surprising, since the base of the pads of the foot become quite hard and

A few dogs don't like being touched very much, either by their owners, other dogs, or people that they don't know. Sometimes this may be caused by a negative experience—discomfort at the vets, for example. However, more commonly it is caused by a lack of experience. Such dogs need to have their confidence improved by a gradual, careful behavioral program.

calloused from walking on hard surfaces and lose some of their sensitivity to touch. However, the other areas are all prime sites for touch communication between dogs, and so are likely to be sensitive to the human touch as well.

Teaching your dog to cope with being touched all over is vital—whether or not your dog is touch-sensitive. Early handling is associated with pleasant things, such as food or games, and helps a puppy understand that even firm restraint is nothing to be afraid of.

Dogs touch each other during social interaction, and often when sleeping. Dogs that get along well together are more likely to seek out the comfort of another dog's touch when resting—to share body warmth and security, just as they did when pups.

below: *Visual communication is the first option in dog language.*

the social **dog**

above: *Sentry duty.*

right: *Dogs retain juvenile playfulness even into old age.*

From hunting to guarding its territory, from communicating within the pack and between species to its reproductive practices, the dog is a social animal.

the communicating dog

Dogs are pack animals. This means that they live among others of their own species, instead of on their own. In the wild, a pack may be as few as two individuals or as many as 10 or 12. In cases where large numbers of animals share the same space and resources, good communication systems need to be created and used to minimize conflict.

Of course, as in any social group, disputes between members sometimes occur. However, physical aggression or direct force is rarely used, as it carries the risk of injury. Losing even one member to injury may reduce the pack's hunting success, and this in turn may affect the ability to raise puppies and perpetuate the pack's genes.

In order to reduce the risk of fights and disputes, dogs have evolved sophisticated communication. Of course, they do not use words or sentences to speak to each other, but they have an effective system of visual signals, olfactory signals, auditory cues, and touch-related signs that tell members of their own species about mood, intention, status, and even hormonal states.

Canine communication systems can be very subtle—from a raised eyebrow or a quick glance, to more obvious signs, such as bared teeth or a tail raised high into the air. Dogs that have been raised in a litter and have had social contact with their mother and other adult dogs learn the basics of dog language by the time they are around 12 weeks of age. Of course, they continue to develop their own use of the language and learn more social skills after this time—but these first weeks are absolutely essential.

Dogs are not born knowing which signals to use or what their mother's body postures mean. They need to learn them, just like children learn a spoken language—and the constant refinement of the use of this language is a life-long lesson.

below: *All puppies need to learn to understand the "canine language"—and become fluent themselves.*

man and dog—speaking to each other across the centuries

One of the reasons why dogs and man have become such close companions must be that our communication systems are remarkably similar. Both man and dog have ritualized some aspects of aggression, so that contests can take place without the risk of harm to either party. Dogs spend a great deal of time playing—even if food or shelter is in short supply—and this not only hones their hunting skills, but also gives them the opportunity to reaffirm who is strongest, fastest, or most ingenious in obtaining and keeping various resources, such as food. Does man do the same? Just think of a football game—the similarities are obvious!

However, the very fact that dogs have communication systems that closely resemble ours has been their greatest torment, as well as their most important asset. Clearly, dogs do not know English or any other language. They cannot understand the meanings of any words we say, yet because dogs are such excellent observers, they often interpret our body language to match the sound of the spoken word. Sadly, this can give the impression that the dog understands our conversation, and can lead to great misunderstandings between the canine and human involved.

Understanding just how dogs see the world, how they communicate, and how they can learn to translate our words is an educational experience well worth pursuing. Your dog will thank you for it.

pack structure

In a wild pack of dogs, a social system or hierarchy is in place. This is primarily to ensure that order is kept within the group and that "decisions," such as when to go hunting, are made and supported by the pack as a team.

Teamwork has many benefits. The greatest of these is that a pack can hunt and bring down much larger prey than dogs that hunt alone or in small groups. Teamwork also reduces the amount of energy that needs to be expended per hunt, and maximizes the amount of time and resources that the pack will then have for raising young.

Establishing a "rank order" or "pecking order" in the team means

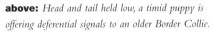

above: Head and tail held low, a timid puppy is offering deferential signals to an older Border Collie.

that each member knows his or her role and will perform it without question—answering to the leader at all times. However, this is not a dictatorship, and there is some flexibility in the hierarchy. This theory equates well to an efficient human commercial company. The executive director may have overall control, but he cannot run the organization without the support and input of the workers, supervisors, and so on. Equally, some of those workers may have their eye on promotion, and if they can show that they have the ability and commitment to the work, they may find that they are given extra pay or privileges.

It is thought that domestic dogs have retained at least 75 percent of all wolf traits. However, domestication has altered their "ambitions" and left them in a permanently junior state. This is

left: An adult disciplines an exuberant pup.

just as well for us, because it means that the dog's drive to compete for resources and breeding rights is dramatically reduced. In a family home, where one or two dogs live with people, and possibly other animals, such as cats or rabbits, their wild instincts have been sufficiently tamed.

However, there can be occasions when a dog starts to behave as if it has been given the rights of the executive director and has ambitions for a platinum card! Such dogs are not truly "dominant." Dominance in a canine pack is intended to clearly define breeding rights—and it is highly unlikely that domestic dogs look upon us, as the rest of their pack, in that way. Instead, these dogs have discovered that

life is full of rewards—getting up on the sofa when they want to, going out for a walk when they choose, even forcing their owners to pet them on demand. Such dogs are usually bright—they have discovered that human beings are easy to train as long as they are persistent and that behaviors such as barking, pawing, whining, or scratching at the door work every time.

Sadly, some of these dogs also realize that the use of aggressive displays—or even biting—can be effective in getting what they want, when they want it, so they become aggressive toward their owners. Such dogs are usually fast learners, which means that they can learn to behave like lower-ranking members again. However, a carefully

prepared behavioral program is necessary in such cases in order to avoid further conflict.

For most dogs, basic house rules suffice to prevent any such problems. Consistency about what the dog is allowed to do, and when it may do it, ensures that the whole family treats the dog fairly and that household disputes among the humans are kept to a minimum. Dogs are part of our families and can make wonderful friends, companions, and working partners—but a dog can also resemble a spoiled child if basic boundaries are not maintained.

below: *Working Sheepdogs demonstrating social signals.*

above: *Getting ready for play—ear and tail positions give information about mood and intention.*

visual signals

Dogs use a multitude of visual signals to indicate their emotional state and behavioral intentions. Learning to interpret these signals is a little like learning a new language. Individually, each signal has a meaning that can be compared to a dictionary definition. However, once these signals are put together, they can convey whole chapters of meaning.

facial expression

Dogs use facial expression a great deal in even simple, everyday communication. Some of these signals are quite subtle, while others are more obvious. Dogs use their eyes, ears, mouth, lips, teeth, and even their foreheads to convey information.

eyes

A dog's eyes can convey a great deal of information. Generally, averting the eyes is a signal that indicates the dog is non-threatening. In contrast to a head-on stare, turning the face away, putting the ears back, and even licking the lips slightly is a pacifying or appeasement gesture, designed to say, "I'm friendly and non-threatening." If understood, it allows free and friendly communication between dogs or dogs and people, with each individual turning their face away alternately.

Direct eye contact can be regarded as a challenge. However, some breeds of dog that have been bred to use eye contact, to herd sheep, for example, actually find direct eye contact rewarding—and positively enjoy it.

ears

Ears are often an excellent barometer of a dog's feelings and intentions. Ears up and alert often indicate excitement, confidence, or assertion, while ears that are held back and down usually indicate submission or fear. Ears turned almost inside out can show exuberance or flirtation.

However, while reading such meaning into the ear positions of, say, a German Shepherd may be relatively simple, human interference through selective breeding may make interpretation more difficult. For example, short-nosed, or brachycephalic, breeds such as Boxers or French Bulldogs, which are wrinkled around the facial area, with short muzzles and rounded eyes, may look as though they are showing assertion, or even aggression, particularly if their breathing is labored.

Even more difficult to read are those breeds that look permanently submissive. For example, Cocker Spaniels tend to have doleful eyes and long, drooping ears. Even if they are feeling anxious, aggressive, or assertive, they may not appear so, leaving few warning signals available.

mouth, lips, and teeth

The dog's use of its mouth, lips, and teeth to demonstrate submission, confidence, fear, or assertion are fundamentally important. A dog that is relaxed and confident is likely to have relaxed facial muscles. The mouth may hang slightly open, and the tongue may protrude slightly.

A dog that is anxious or fearful is likely to use its mouth in a different way. By drawing the lips back, almost into a grin, the teeth are still concealed, but the face becomes narrow and the eyes form into slits. The dog's tongue may come out to lick. Licking tends to be a submissive behavior that harks back to when the dog was a puppy and solicited food from its mother in this way.

Conversely, a dog that is showing

Some dogs are known to "smile" or "grin," and this is quite different from a dog that is snarling. This is a submissive or pacifying gesture and clearly resembles our interpretation of a true smile. The dog may draw back both lips, but keeps its teeth hidden. Sometimes, the corners of the mouth may even be drawn into an upward curve—just like a human grin. This trait seems to be a breed-specific characteristic— Dalmatians and Golden Retrievers are classic smilers, although there is undoubtedly a learned element to the behavior.

dominance, or even aggression, is likely to make its face look as large and powerful as possible. One of the clearest facial expressions that a dog can give is snarling: lips drawn back to expose the front teeth, muzzle wrinkled upward, ears forward, and eyes staring—this dog is obviously saying "keep away." While there can be little doubt that this is an aggressive display, it is indeed only a display, designed to avoid further conflict or the risk of injury. Only if the warning goes unheeded will the dog need to escalate its aggression.

body posture

In addition to facial expression, dogs use their whole bodies to communicate with others. These signals indicate playfulness, anxiety, confidence, or aggression to other dogs—and they try to use them with us, too. Learning to speak "canine" will improve your relationship with your dog.

below: *A clear visual display—ears back, eyes wide and staring, and teeth bared.*

the play-bow

One of the most misunderstood body signals dogs use is the play-bow, because humans often interpret this as the dog preparing to attack them. This classic pose—bottom in the air, with tail held high, head right down to the ground—is one of the most commonly used signals between dogs to indicate their intention to play. Such signals are vitally important, as they reassure the other dog that no threat is intended.

giving paw

Many of us pride ourselves on training our dogs to give a paw as a trick—little knowing that the dog practiced the behavior in the nest. Within only a few hours, newborn puppies knead their mother's nipples with their front paws to stimulate the milk flow. This later becomes a supplicating gesture

that puppies use to indicate their submission to their mother. This is then easily transferred to us, as substitute mothers, when the puppy comes into its new home.

Dogs often use "floppy elbow"

above: *Play is an essential component of canine communication systems.*

below: *Different breeds signal in different ways. Early social experience helps to define these varying "dialects."*

gestures to initiate play between themselves—a puppy's raised paw is a clear indication of a desire to have a game with another dog. However, in adult dogs, a paw placed on the back or shoulders of another dog may not be quite so innocent. Such behavior may be interpreted as an attempt to dominate—or even to mount.

rolling over

Dogs roll onto their backs for lots of reasons. Certainly, this gesture can mean submission—the dog is demonstrating its total acquiescence to another dog or person by placing itself in the most vulnerable position possible.

A dog in this classic passive submission pose usually shows narrowed eyes, ears flattened to the head, lips drawn back, and tail tucked between the legs. Dogs that really need to emphasize their subservience may also leak a few drops of urine—for the other dog to sniff—and may fan the scent of it by flicking the end of their tail back and forth.

In play, dogs of relatively equal status will experiment with rolling over, while the other dog stands above them. This is usually reversed quite quickly—with the apparent "underdog" using its feet to push its "opponent" away.

wagging tail

Tail wagging means the dog is happy and friendly—doesn't it? Unfortunately, this is not always so. The position of the tail, how fast it is wagging, and in what context reveals a great deal about a dog's intentions— and they are not always positive.

Dogs that hold their tails straight up are usually indicating confidence, assertive behavior, or high excitement. Combine this with a very stiff, fast, and short wag, and the dog may be trying to exert dominance over another dog, or warning a human to go carefully— the dog is prepared to command

respect if it has to. Many of the northern breeds, such as huskies and Akitas, use this posture as a demonstration of confidence among other dogs.

Tails that are held in neutral—that is, in a natural position, level with the body or slightly lower—are usually feeling neutral, too; relaxed, friendly, and secure. Such tail positions may be accompanied by long, graceful swishes of the tail— wagging is slow and relaxed as the tail moves in a wide arc from side to side. Wagging hard at this level also indicates friendliness and excitement in most contexts, and for most breeds it is the tail-wag you see when coming home at the end of the day or when you get out

a toy to play with your dog.

Sadly, many victims of dog aggression report that the dog was wagging its tail when it bit them. The dog was not enjoying being aggressive—it was indicating its uncertainty about the situation. Conversely, a tail that is held low, or even between the legs, is usually indicative of anxiety, uncertainty, or even fear.

Tails are such an important part of canine communication that docked breeds are almost certainly at a disadvantage.

below: *A raised paw is a supplicating gesture learned as a puppy.*

29

left: *Howling can be a "call to arms" or an attempt to reunite the pack. This dog is calling to his absent owners.*

auditory signals

One of the great differences between dogs and their wild ancestors, wolves, is that dogs make much more noise. Wolves rarely bark. However, they are well known for their ability to howl. This vocal signal is used to call together the pack, usually for a hunting

below: *A clear display of aggression. This dog uses ritual signals—bared teeth, narrowed eyes, and ears back—in an attempt to remove the threat.*

trip, and bonds the group before setting out.

The domestic dog has inherited the ability to howl—and some try to call together their family or "pack" by this means if they are left alone at home, although others only howl when prompted by certain sounds—familiar music, for example.

On the whole, domestic dogs tend to use vocalizations in three main ways to communicate: barking, growling, and whining.

barking

Of all the complaints that are made about domestic dogs, barking is probably at the top of the list. Dogs bark for a multitude of reasons, but the primary one is that it usually gets a response.

The most common reason for dogs to bark is as an alarm. A short, loud bark is intended to alert the whole pack, or family, that danger is present and that an intruder is approaching. Of course, if this happens to be the mail carrier, the dog is rewarded for its behavior—because it is also likely to think that it chased the intruder away.

Some dogs bark when excited, and this communicates their joy or pleasure to others. Unfortunately, if they do this while greeting a visitor, it may not be appropriate—and here the owner's and visitor's response is important. Since dogs do not understand the meaning of our words, any shouting is likely to be interpreted as barking encouragement—and will only make matters worse. Some breeds or types of dogs, such as herding dogs, bark at other dogs in excitement. This is often done in an attempt to get the other dog to play.

Barking may also be a sign of insecurity or defensive behavior. Because nearly all aggression is intended to create distance between the dog and the perceived threat, the barking serves to warn others to keep away. If this is successful, the dog may learn that the strategy is effective and will continue to perform this behavior.

growling

Some dogs growl as a part of play. In the same way that we may join in with a football cheer or tease an opponent on the racquetball court, so some dogs use this method of communication during non-threatening competition. Terriers, in particular, are prone to making fierce growling noises when playing with other dogs. These can sound threatening unless the rest of the dog's body language and facial expressions are taken into account.

Apart from play, growling is usually a clear warning from one dog to another, or from a dog to a human. A dog's growl is intended to show the opponent that the dog means business, but would really like to avoid any physical conflict. A dog that is growling at people or other dogs is usually showing some form of behavioral problem. However, it is much better for a dog to use this method of communication as an early warning system than to leave its intentions unclear, then resort to physical aggression. At least the time-bomb can be heard ticking.

whining

Whining can indicate excitement, that the dog is in pain or discomfort, or it can be used as an attention-seeking mechanism. Some dogs learn to whine in order to demand feeding, walks, or petting, as they know it is very hard to ignore. A dog that starts to whine suddenly, steadily, and for no apparent reason may be indicating that it is unwell or in pain. A visit to the vet will put your mind at rest.

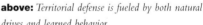

above: *Territorial defense is fueled by both natural drives and learned behavior.*

olfactory signals

Despite the many similarities between the communication systems of dogs and man, there is one area where we have to bow to the dog's superiority. Olfactory, or scent signals, are commonly used throughout the animal kingdom, and especially among social animals.

Unfortunately, because we do not possess the special scenting abilities of the dog, there is much that remains a mystery about how dogs use smell and the kind of information that can be conveyed by it.

left: *An adult wolf greets a puppy. Sniffing is always part of such rituals.*

above: *Fast and furious, this game may look uncontrolled but both dogs are careful to play by ritualized "rules."*

Dogs almost always greet each other by summing each other up visually, then sniffing each other to gather more information from an olfactory source. Glands throughout the body are probably responsible for producing a dog's odor, which is as unique as a fingerprint. Information is probably contained in these chemical messengers that indicates the state of the dog's health, its sex, its hormonal status, and even how confident or assertive it is.

In addition to passing information in this direct fashion, dogs leave scent signals for others to find in their absence. Urine marks left by dogs are "read" like the morning newspaper by others passing by even several hours later, and these dogs may overmark such signals to add their scent to the site.

Both male and female dogs use urine to mark territory and to leave information. Males usually learn to cock their legs during adolescence. This action is supposed to place the urine mark as high as possible on a marker post or site—presumably so that it is as close to head height and as obvious as possible to other dogs, and also to indicate that it has been left by a dog

large enough and fit enough to make such a mark. Bitches usually squat to urinate, although many like to overmark where other dogs have already urinated in the same way as male dogs do. Bitches coming into season also start to advertize their hormonal state by urinating in very small amounts as frequently as possible when outside. This again confirms the theory that urine contains information about gender and sex that other dogs can interpret.

Scent glands contained in the anal sacs, on either side of the anus, also empty onto feces when the dog relieves itself. This leads some male dogs in particular to try to place their feces as high as possible—up on tree stumps, for example—even if it does take some gymnastic movement to get it there!

In addition to such obvious scent signals, it is thought that more subtle olfactory messages are also used by dogs in communication. Pheromones are chemicals produced by the body that

below: *A little unsure, one dog turns his head and faces away from the other.*

are given off in almost indiscernible quantities. Studies of other animals have shown that some of these chemical messengers released into the air can be "read" by others of the same species even hours later. Fear pheromones, particularly, may be powerful enough to remain a long time after the frightened animal has gone—with the ability to affect the behavior of other animals that then enter the area. This has interesting implications for dogs that may come to form a fear of the veterinary clinic or even a training facility if another dog was previously fearful in the same spot. It may also mean that dogs can "translate" human fear pheromones as well, giving some support to the theory that dogs can tell when a person is afraid of them.

touch used in communication

Dogs use touch in their communication with one another, and this varies from the lightest nudge with a muzzle to an overwhelmingly aggressive display.

Most owners already know how much dogs enjoy physical contact. Many pet dogs want to be able to touch their owner for reassurance, comfort, and the confirmation that they are part of the pack. Indeed, in many well-established relationships the dog is just content to be able to rest its head against the owner's knee, or to lie close to the owner's feet.

Generally, dogs enjoy touch that is non-threatening and fits in with their social repertoire. Stroking on the chest, the throat, and the belly is usually favored, while being stroked directly on the head, the back of the neck, or down the back to the tail can be regarded as a little threatening. This is because nearly all canine greeting behaviors are centered around the head and face—puppies learn to ask adult dogs for food by begging around their lips, while social threat or challenge is normally carried out by putting the paws or head over the

neck or back of the other dog.

An exception to this rule are those dogs that like to be touched on the rump, and will turn around and offer their owner or visitor their rear ends in greeting, rather than their heads or faces. While this may seem strange to us, these dogs are clearly saying, "I'm no threat—look, no teeth this end!" Gundogs seem particularly prone to this behavior and will often turn in ecstatic circles if they can encourage the person being greeted to scratch them on the rump at the same time.

Dogs that like to use this submissive strategy to greet people may find it difficult to behave naturally when restrained on a leash. In a situation where turning is not possible, they may attempt to jump up at the person, or if told to sit, may wriggle and writhe in frustration. While many good training classes advocate "sit to greet" as the ideal behavior, for these dogs it may be more difficult.

If you have a dog that rushes to greet you or visitors at the front door and is likely to jump up, establishing a new greeting strategy based on this behavior may be effective, particularly if your dog likes to carry things in its

above: *Nearly all domestic dogs enjoy physical contact with their owners.*

mouth. Sending the dog to get a toy, then allowing the dog to move back to the visitor naturally, ignoring any unwanted behavior and rewarding calm, friendly behavior, works well.

Although physical conflict is usually avoided in canine communication, where it does occur, injury rarely results. This is because even in a fight dogs have social rules that they adhere to—one of which is to use bite inhibition; to bite without breaking the skin. Dogs use jaws and paws as primary weapons in a physical contest. The majority of dogs attempt to make their opponent submit by rolling them onto their backs—usually by knocking them with their body weight then standing over them. The victor is then likely to use its jaws to pin the other dog to the ground, although no actual biting injury results. Such aggression would usually be the "last resort" where other communication has previously failed.

freedom of speech

Being able to read a foreign language is very nice, but if you can't speak it, communication is much reduced. Although it is important to know what your dog is trying to tell you, using signals that your dog understands—especially body language and facial expressions—means that you will be able to talk to your dog.

Dogs are primarily visual creatures. This means that although they learn to interpret the words that we use to mean "come," "sit," or "stay," the rest of our words and conversations must be a little like listening to background music—you know it's there, but there is no need to pay attention to it. Using clear body postures and facial expressions to convey your meanings will cut through the background noise of everyday life and give your dog a chance to concentrate on what you are saying. Owners and trainers who use such methods quickly find that they need to do less and less interpretation—dog and human really

above: *All domestic dogs need to learn the basics of social manners.*

are speaking the same language.

Unfortunately, some of our body language and behavior must seem very strange to our dogs. For example, when we are happy and content, we smile—which involves showing our teeth. Human smiling is one area where canine and human language can become difficult to translate, and dogs need to learn that showing our teeth when smiling is non-threatening. They probably do this during the socialization period—where they watch the rest of our body language and the context in which we smile and figure out that a display of human

left: *Possession is all in dog "law." This puppy rolls his eyes to indicate slight uncertainy on someone's approach.*

teeth often means good things are coming. Perhaps our lack of large canine teeth, or fangs, also helps. Certainly, dogs quickly pick up on smiling as a friendly human gesture—many dogs will wag their tails, get up, or come for attention at the merest hint of their owner smiling at them.

Conversely, there are many behaviors that dogs offer that we can easily misinterpret. The most common of these is an expression of "guilt." Guilt is a human emotion, not shared by animals, yet the body language that dogs show when they are fearful can easily appear to reflect an interpretation of our own emotions.

Imagine that you have left your dog home alone. You have been out for only a couple of hours, but on your return you discover that your dog has chewed your best furniture. It bounds toward the front door to greet you as normal, but can immediately tell that you are not in a good mood. Even if you do not use physical punishment,

above: *This puppy avoids his owner's stare by looking directly ahead. All pups need to learn that such human facial expressions are non-threatening.*

your dog will know that you are angry by reading your body language and facial expression—but it will not understand why.

If this happens several times, your dog may start to anticipate your mysterious aggression on your return home and will prepare for it by showing submissive body language as soon as it hears your key in the lock. Ears back, head down, and tail between its legs is a posture interpreted as guilt; actually, your dog is reacting to unprovoked and irrational anger. Sadly, many dogs learn to react this way—and some then start to chew more through anxiety, doubling the problem.

Dogs never lie about the way they are feeling. Many of their communication systems are open to misinterpretation by their owners, so with just a little understanding and education in dog language your relationship can be greatly enhanced for life.

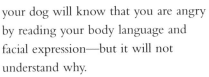

left: *Intent on gazing at her owner's face, this puppy whines in anticipation.*

the territorial dog

Wolves and wild dogs live in clearly defined areas, known as the pack territory. Within this territory, all the individuals know each another and are able to recognize each other through sight and smell. Pack territory is heavily guarded, because keeping possession of the best hunting grounds, the ideal resting sites, and the most secure dens for breeding is important to the survival of the group. Elaborate rituals are used to mark the edges of this territory—using urine and feces to scent-mark on a frequent basis.

Other groups in the same area may attempt to steal such resources if they get the chance, and this means that pack members are always looking for unknown dogs that may be competitors. If such an intruder is sighted, the pack is called to arms and the leader decides whether the individual should be driven away.

Such determined social behavior in the dog's ancestors and wild cousins suggests that our domestic pets also regard their own home and property as their territory, and this is borne out when they behave in ways designed to repel "intruders," until told to do otherwise by their human leaders. Dogs often bark at boundary points, to warn others away. The front gate, the front door, or the garden fence are all common sites for aggression to visitors in dogs that have taken their role as "early warning system" just one step too far for our needs.

Interestingly, dogs that are taken to the same places for exercise are also likely to count this as their territory—or perhaps as their hunting ground. Here, domestic dogs follow all the same rituals to mark their territory—urine marking and leaving feces as frequently as possible along the walk.

These similarities make the fact that most pet dogs can meet and greet other dogs on the same street without fighting even more remarkable. Thankfully, the breeding of our domestic dogs, combined with early socialization, means that they are usually playful with others and do not regard them as competitors.

In order to make this sociability possible, domestic dogs use strict rules when meeting others, to emphasize the fact they do not represent a threat or a challenge to another dog's resources. Dogs spend a great deal of time sniffing the urine marks left by other dogs, and this probably gives them prior warning of who is in the park, and how familiar they are.

Once within visual range, dogs take a little time to sum each other up. Most approach at a slight angle, rather than straight toward each other, which could be regarded as a threat. When in close proximity, sniffing usually takes place—often around the facial area first, then the rear end, where the scent glands are most productive. If the dogs are going to play, one or the other will make a clear signal of intention—such as a play-bow, a paw lift, or a pounce. If the dogs are going to pass in a more dignified manner, one will often walk away, cock his leg to urinate, then move off.

Ideally, domestic dogs should not be allowed to form strong territorial behaviors around the house, yard, or the park, as this can lead to unnecessary conflict. Neutering male dogs dramatically reduces this drive, and early socialization is also vital to ensuring that your dog does not think he owns the park.

opposite page: *Most male dogs scent-mark using urine when out for walks. This leaves olfactory information for other dogs in the area.*

right: *Teaching a young dog to accept visitors to the home is a vital part of its training.*

the sociable dog

The importance of social living for all dogs cannot be underestimated. A true pack animal, the dog relies almost entirely on the support of its pack-mates for protection, company, and food.

Litters of puppies in a wild dog pack nearly always contain several pups. The average number in a litter is eight, and they are cared for by their mother in a secure den. Other pack members bring the mother food during this time, and help to raise the puppies when they emerge from their underground nest. After this time, all the pack members interact with the growing pups—teaching them about pack rules, as well as helping them to practice hunting skills through play. Once fully grown, the pack's investment pays off, as the new adults assist in hunting expeditions and provide food for a new litter in their turn.

In this way, wild dogs living in a communal pack spend all of their time together. They eat, sleep, hunt, and even play together—and this increases the bond between them. There are very few times when a wild dog finds itself alone. From the moment it is born to the moment it dies, it has pack members nearby.

Occasionally, a dog's behavior may be so unruly that the rest of the pack ignore it. This rejection usually does the trick, but if not, they may drive the dog away and off their territory. If this individual is a young bitch who will soon come into season, she may have a chance of meeting another pack and being accepted by them. However, as often happens, the exiled individual is likely to die.

This reliance on the pack for food and support has great implications for our domestic dogs. Although we can teach them to cope with being by themselves, this is not a natural state, and requires practice and early experience. Many domestic dogs suffer from "separation anxiety" as a result of poor early learning—and howl, bark, or cry when left alone. Such dogs may also vent their frustration by becoming destructive, or urinating and defecating in the home. This is not misbehavior, but real distress at being separated from the rest of the pack. Early and

below: *The freedom to run and play with other dogs is the canine equivalent of leisure time.*

above: *All puppies use biting in play. They need to learn to control this habit around humans.*

effective behavioral help is needed for such dogs. It is rarely useful to buy the dog a canine companion, as it is the adult family members that the dog has the firmest attachment to, not another juvenile pack member.

In addition to food, shelter, and protection from predators, most dog packs value social interaction very highly. Social interaction can be subtle and calm. Even tiny signals, such as eye contact and sniffing, act as communication between dogs, and can lead to bonds between individuals in a pack that equate well to human "friendships." Indeed, it has been shown that gaining a relationship with a higher ranking individual can increase protection for a lower one, so it is worth being nice to the boss sometimes.

Play is a very important activity—and increases the depth of social bonding between pack members. It also serves to hone hunting skills and teaches individuals about each other's strengths and weaknesses. In a wild dog or wolf pack even the adults set aside large amounts of time for play, which indicates how important it is to pack cohesion. Perhaps the expression "those that play together, stay together" really is true in this instance.

Understanding the social dynamics of a wild dog pack helps us to see how our domestic dogs view life in our homes and families. Many of the interactions that dogs use with each

play by the rules

■ Human slavery has officially been abolished—but not according to many dogs. Play or interaction needs to be when you decide, not at the whim of the dog. Although many of us enjoy our pets asking for attention, it can become a nuisance if they pester us at mealtimes, annoy visitors, or repeatedly throw toys at us while we are watching television. Consistency is the key. If you feel like having a game, a grooming session, or a walk with your dog, call it to you and let it know. Open arms, a smiling face, and pleasant noises, such as calling or even clapping, can indicate that you would like to interact. Alternatively, if your dog pesters you for attention at an inappropriate time, switch off immediately. Close your body language by folding your arms, look away rather than toward your dog, and stay silent. This acts as a stop signal to the dog and it will start to learn what that means.

■ Keep a special toy that you and your dog play with—rather than ones it's allowed to have at other times. This makes the game more exciting.

■ Bear in mind that dogs are predators—the more the toy acts like "prey," the more exciting it will be. Rather than throwing the toy or giving it to the dog, making it move quickly and erratically along the ground will probably be more enticing.

■ When reaching for a toy that your dog is holding, watch its body language and facial expression. If it stands still, dips the head downward, or turns the head away, the dog may be uncertain about giving up possession. Always reach for the toy from under the dog's chin, until you can predict its behavior, as this is less threatening. Offer something in exchange if necessary—such as another toy or a treat.

■ Use play in training as much as possible. For every exercise that your dog performs well in the early stages of training, its needs to be richly rewarded. This means playing with a toy for ten minutes if your dog has managed a one-minute sit-stay. You are never wasting your time rewarding your dog in this way.

Dogs love social interaction. Without it they can become bored, lonely, and "depressed," and in the wild can even die. In these days of hard work, time commitments, space restrictions, and the dispersal of family groups and supportive friendships, dogs offer us the unusual opportunity to interact with another social being without conditions. Enjoy!

other can be used by humans with their dogs, if applied in the right ways. Play, for example, is very important in creating a strong relationship between you and your pet dog. No matter what the breed or type, a willingness to play using toys shows that you have a common understanding. However, in order to make sure that your dog appreciates the difference between a game and a contest of strength or a battle of wills, a few basic rules need to be followed (see above).

the hunting dog

Even the most gentle lap dog has its origins in the great hunting ancestors of the dog. While few domestic dogs now have to hunt for their food, the drive to do so remains in nearly all breeds, to some extent.

In a wild state, dogs obtain food in three main ways. The first of these is by scavenging. Wild dogs and wolves eat berries, eggs, the remains of dead animals that they find, and even some vegetation. Although the type of food available depends on the environment and the time of year, they are able to utilize a wide number of food sources in this way.

However, dogs need protein, and the most concentrated source is from the meat of other animals. In order to obtain this, dogs also go hunting. In a pack situation, this is most likely to be carried out using organized teamwork. After setting off on a hunt, the dogs are likely to split up in order to fulfill different roles. One dog may be used to find the prey, another to circle around the prey, while other dogs follow up the rear, or cut off the animal's escape.

The dogs come together as the hunt is in progress, chasing down an animal, and using their combined bodyweight to bring it to the ground. Once there, it may take several of them to hold it down and kill it, so each pack member needs to rely on its teammates not to let go. Such hunting expeditions are not always successful, and although they are likely to provide meat for many individuals at the same time, they require the expenditure of a great deal of energy.

above right: *The weapons of a true predator, the dog's teeth are designed for tearing and crushing.*

the dog's teeth

Adult dogs have a total of 42 teeth. Incisors are for cutting, the canines for tearing, and the molars for crushing. Some breeds have missing dentition, as the shape of their jaw or head can no longer accommodate a full set.

Incisors	Upper jaw – 6	Lower jaw – 6
Canines	Upper jaw – 2	Lower jaw – 2
Premolars	Upper jaw – 8	Lower jaw – 8
Molars	Upper jaw – 4	Lower jaw – 6

At other times, dogs in a wild pack may go hunting for small quarry by themselves. Wild dogs eat rabbits, birds if they can catch them, and small rodents, such as mice, as well as some large insects.

All three of these methods for obtaining food are echoed in the behavior of our domestic dogs today. Dogs are very successful scavengers. Feral packs can live almost entirely from the waste they find in human trash cans and refuse sites, and even in our homes we can see how strongly this drive remains. Few domestic dogs ignore food dropped on the floor. Many beg for food at human mealtimes, and a large percentage also make use of any bits or pieces of edible matter that they find while out on walks or lurking in the kitchen trash can.

Although most dogs receive free food from us two to three times a day, many still retain a pack hunting instinct that they demonstrate in other ways. Chasing balls or toys and bringing them back is one outlet, as are other games, such as hide-and-seek or two dogs chasing each other.

On some occasions it is also possible to see two or more dogs from the same household attempting to round up or "hunt" other dogs, people, birds, or animals in the park or yard. Thankfully, the end stage of this hunting sequence has been inhibited by thousands of years of domestication—but the "eye, stalk, chase" part is still inherently satisfying for the dog.

Finally, the solo hunting skills of the wild dog looking for a snack are still alive and well in our pet dogs. "Mouse pouncing" is a common play behavior. This is where the dog stares intently at something on the ground—a toy, or even an insect—and rears the front of its body up in one great elevation, then pounces with both front feet onto the "quarry" below.

below: *Cape Hunting Dogs share the kill. Teamwork is the essence of such hunting.*

the reproductive dog

One of the major differences between domestic dogs and wild dogs such as wolves is that they breed more prolifically. Wolves have only one opportunity to breed each year, and although there are some notable exceptions, most domestic bitches come into season twice a year. Males are ready to mate at any time!

A bitch's first season, which

above: *The bitch indicates her readiness to mate by putting her tail to one side.*

indicates the onset of sexual maturity, can occur any time between six and 18 months of age, although between eight and 13 months is more common. A season usually lasts about three weeks.

Before the bitch is fertile, the womb prepares for possible puppies and sheds its lining—causing bleeding to occur. Bleeding may last from four days to two weeks. During this time, the bitch's scent is highly attractive to males, but she is not ready to mate, so she may be snappy in order to keep them at bay. After the bleeding finishes, the bitch is usually fertile for between five and 12 days.

courtship rituals

Most bitches are quite clear about whether or not they are ready to mate with a dog and most require ritual

left: *Taking the opportunity!*

left: *A young pup's face is dominated by its nose! The sense of smell is most important at this age.*

Several "primitive" breeds, such as the basenji, come into season only once a year, instead of twice like most domestic dogs. Even more unusually, some males in one or two breeds retract their testicles until the females come into heat.

courtship before allowing any advances. Much sniffing and licking usually takes place and the two dogs may play together. When she is ready to mate, the bitch will stand still and communicate her willingness by putting her tail on one side. The male then clasps the female with his forelegs around her middle. Ejaculation of semen usually occurs within one minute—but the mating is far from over. At this point, a bulbous area at the base of the dog's penis, called the bulbourethral gland, swells with blood. This enlarges to such an extent that it is impossible to separate the male and female for between five and 30 minutes, during which time the dogs may maneuver themselves so that they stand back-to-back until separation occurs.

In a natural state, the mother would dig a large den in which to have her pups. Gestation usually takes 63 days. Once born, the pups are totally dependent on their mother until they are ready to emerge from the den when they are about four weeks old. Other members of the pack then help in their rearing and bring food for both the puppies and the mother.

Domestic dogs usually mate and give birth naturally. A Caesarean section is sometimes required if the bitch is in trouble or the breed's offspring have such large heads that a natural birth is impossible. Newborn puppies have no control over their body temperature, so it is vital that they huddle together for warmth as soon as possible and find a nipple from which to suckle.

Pups are born blind and deaf, and although they can move by using a "swimming" action, with their front feet paddling to pull them along the ground, they cannot walk. Their eyes usually open after about 14 days, while their ears are not fully functional until they are three to four weeks of age, by which time the puppies are able to walk, run, and pick themselves up when they fall down.

Of course, few puppies are raised by any dog other than their mothers in breeders' homes. Where other dogs do have contact with the puppies they can teach them much about canine language and their role in the pack.

below: *Newborn puppies are blind and deaf, but they are adept at finding a teat and keeping warm.*

the athletic dog

Watch a dog herding sheep, being agile, or simply chasing a ball in the backyard, and you will see a harmony of strong bone, stretching muscle, and internal systems that allow for great flexibility, speed, and balance.

the dog's skeleton

The dog's skeleton supports and protects the body's internal organs. Bones are hollow tubes, made up of a latticed structure of hard, calcified struts, filled in the center with bone marrow. Blood vessels nourish this living structure by entering the bone through tiny holes. This allows a broken bone to regrow and mend itself.

Unlike humans, dogs do not have a collar bone. The forelimbs are held in place by muscles alone. This allows the dog greater agility in running, jumping, swimming, and turning.

the muscular system

Muscles are made up of fibers that contract when stimulated by a nerve impulse. The ends of the muscles are attached to bone by tendons. This means that the contraction and relaxation of a muscle causes movement in the joints, allowing them to bend, extend, move inward, outward, or rotate. Each muscle is opposed by another that exerts the opposite effect.

Muscles have a number of functions in the canine body. Not only are they responsible for movement, but they also provide protection for the vital organs and bones. In addition, they generate body heat by causing shivering, and allow respiration, defecation, and birth. They also make up the bulk of heart tissue.

Dogs are able to walk, trot, canter, and gallop, as well as jump, twist, swim, and even crawl. The gait that the dog chooses is likely to depend on its motivation and the purpose of the movement, as well as the dog's breed or type. For example, large breeds often choose to lope in an extended walk, while the smaller, more sprightly breeds may show a high-stepping, almost hackneyed trot.

In general, dogs do not expend energy unless they have to. This means that the wolf and most domestic dogs favor the trot if attempting to cover long distances, as it has good forward momentum, without burning unnecessary reserves of energy. Sled dogs, such as huskies and Malamutes,

below: *Agility, speed, and tenacity are all required by the Border Collie herding sheep.*

are the long-distance experts. Traveling at a speed of up to 25 mph (40km/h), a thousand miles can be traveled in less than 10 days.

Galloping is used when a short burst of high speed is necessary. This pace uses a large amount of energy and cannot be maintained over long periods. Breeds such as the sight-hounds are the sprinters of the dog world and can reach great speeds over short distances.

Flexibility is also important for many dogs. Some can turn in the air to catch a ball or even a bird, while others can squeeze themselves into narrow underground burrows and are still able to turn while inside. Herding types have been bred to turn quickly while running at the same time. Collies and other herders can also drop to the ground then spring back into action at the slightest signal.

adaptability

Dogs are usually good swimmers. Although it may take a few attempts for a dog to become confident in the water, once familiar with the idea, most really enjoy going for a swim. Some breeds have been specially bred to swim. The Newfoundland, for example, even has webbed feet to assist self-propulsion in the water.

Perhaps the only skill that domestic dogs have not mastered is climbing. Although a few breeds, such as the Affenpinscher, are reputed to be able to climb out of enclosures, such skills are rare. Dogs trained for working trials competitions are required to clear a six-foot (1.8m) vertical wall, called the scale, but most do this by scrambling, using body strength, rather than climbing as a cat would do.

right: *Jumping is a part of most dogs' athletic repertoire.*

the intelligent dog

From the moment they are born to the moment they die, dogs are always learning. Of course, just like us, dogs find it somewhat easier to learn new behaviors when they are young, but this does not mean that elderly dogs cannot learn new things. You can, in fact, "teach an old dog new tricks"!

Dogs of all ages are constantly engaged in trying to learn a foreign language—human. Despite the fact that they are so good at reading our body language and facial expressions, the majority of the words that we use are completely incomprehensible to them.

Those words that dogs do learn to pick up on are signals that mean that something good is about to occur. In this way, the word "walk" may become associated with the leash being produced and the dog being taken out for a walk. After only a few repetitions, the dog becomes excited at the mere suggestion.

However, even in everyday life, dogs learn to do much more complex tasks than simply associating words with actions. Some dogs are so highly trained that they make even long strings of tasks look simple. For example, some dogs that are trained to assist disabled

people can be given money and a list and can go into a store by themselves, offer the money, and bring back items to their owner waiting outside. Such behavior requires flexibility if there's a line of people waiting to be served, for example, and cannot simply be learned by rote because the layout of the store, the height of the counter, etc., may be different each time. This sort of learning requires fairly sophisticated cognitive ability.

It is commonly thought that dogs, like many other animals, learn by trial and error. However, new thinking on the way that animals process information tends to lean toward the idea that this learning should really be called "trial and success."

Put simply, dogs repeat behaviors that they find rewarding. And they are likely to stop performing behaviors that have no rewards, or that result in something unpleasant. This is worth remembering, because the key to effective training, and to solving behavioral problems, is to ask yourself exactly what rewards the dog is getting for the behavior in question.

Rewards come in many different forms and are defined by their effect. For some dogs, a pat on the head and a gentle smile from their owner is a reward worth working for, while for others only food or games with toys will do. Unfortunately, the types of rewards that some dogs will work for lead to misunderstanding and confusion between them and their owners.

Many dogs regard attention—any

left: *Puppies learn very quickly. Gentle, reward-based training should be started as soon as possible.*

opposite page: *Social reinforcement through praise and touch can be a powerful reward.*

attention—from people as rewarding. This means that a behavior that results in attention from an owner or someone else is likely to be repeated, even if the attention is not particularly pleasant. Indeed, for some dogs, being shouted at, told off, or even smacked, is better than nothing at all. This results in the dog behaving in a way that the owner finds annoying or "bad"—in order to receive eye contact, vocal contact, and physical contact—and for the satisfaction of seeing the owner get steamed up and hot under the collar.

Finding out exactly what kinds of rewards your dog will work for is an integral part of both formal and social training. If your dog will sell his soul for a small piece of cheese or liver, this can act as his "salary" for a job well done. If he prefers toys, games, or attention, these should be his rewards.

Very few human beings go to work every day for no pay. Dogs are just the same. If given the right motivation and sufficient reward, their ability to learn will astound you. Give "accidental" rewards for the "wrong" behavior and you could have an evil genius on your hands.

reward systems

Interestingly, it is not only the type of reward that you offer your dog for performing an appropriate behavior that matters, but when you offer it, too.

Much research has been done on this subject, using a wide variety of animals, and even people, to prove that the timing of a reward, and how often it is used, is crucial to learning potential.

Imagine that you perform a set task each and every day at work. At the end of each week you receive a set amount of money as your salary. You are satisfied with what you receive, but it is not very exciting—you know exactly what you will get each and every time. If someone then asked you to do more work or a bigger project for the same amount, you would probably not be very pleased.

However, now imagine that you go to work every day and that your pay is performance-related. You are likely to work harder and faster if you want the reward of more money at the end of the week.

In the same way, dogs that are "paid" exactly the same amount in terms of attention or treats will not want to improve their performance, unless they know that more "pay" is being offered for doing so. They are unlikely to find the same reward very exciting. Varying the type and amount of reward can

make a huge difference.

For example, for us, putting money into a softdrink machine to get a soft drink is the equivalent of expending a little effort and receiving a small, standard reward. Think how much more exciting it is to put your money into a slot machine at the casino. You have no idea what will come out—will it be a small reward, a huge jackpot, or nothing at all? This is known as a variable reward schedule and is extremely powerful. Indeed, it is one of the reasons why gambling is so addictive and why playing the lottery is so popular.

Using rewards in this way in training can be very effective. If your dog has already learned to sit on command, start to make the behavior performance-related for an improvement in speed of response. Once this has been perfected, put the reward on a variable schedule—sometimes a pat, sometimes a food treat, and sometimes nothing at all. Your dog will become highly

above: *A good mother will provide security and gentle discipline.*

left: *Play is a vital part of a young dog's education. Only through such interaction will they learn canine communication systems.*

motivated and will try even harder.

Of course, this can also work in reverse. If you are accidentally rewarding your dog for a behavior that you do not like, a continuous stream of rewards is likely to maintain it, but it is not exciting or addictive. If, on the other hand your dog sometimes receives rewards for the behavior and sometimes doesn't, it could be playing "the lottery."

A good example of this is dogs that beg for food at human mealtimes. If the dog is given tidbits each and every time, it will expect and anticipate the reward. This means that if you decide to stop, the dog will continue to beg for a few days, but is then likely to give up. Alternatively, if it is receiving rewards for begging on an intermittent basis—the children feed it under the table when Mom's not looking, for example—the dog will beg persistently, even when food is not offered, in the hope that its luck will change.

Dogs and humans learn about the world in very similar ways. Early experiences of what is and is not rewarding can form associations for the rest of the dog's life, and can be difficult to alter later on. Making the most of those early weeks of training and socialization can make or break your dog's desire and ability to learn.

above: *Puppies can learn to accept all kinds of animals if introduced early enough.*

below: *Some breeds are more "independent" than others, which makes sufficient motivation even more important in training.*

learning from Mom

Dogs are a wonderful combination of nature and nurture. Obviously, they inherit behavioral characteristics from their parents, in the same way that they inherit physical ones. However, early experiences can shape and develop these characteristics—bringing them to the fore, or concealing them, for the rest of the dog's life.

Newborn puppies are designed to maximize their chances of survival. They eat and sleep in order to grow as rapidly as possible, and this means suckling from their mother as often as they can. However, at around four weeks of age, the bitch usually starts to limit the amount of time that she allows the pups to drink. This is to protect her own physical well-being and also to start the puppies on their road to independence, through weaning.

Although weaning is generally thought of as a physical process, the behavioral effects of learning that milk is not always available are vitally important. Puppies need to learn that

above: *Initially, all of life's rewards come from the puppies' mother. Soon, however, they must learn that food comes from an external source* **(below)**.

they cannot always have food or attention on demand, and their mother's first rejection of them teaches this in a gentle way.

To begin with, the bitch is likely to simply walk away from the puppies—while they clamber after her, trying to reach her teats. Having failed, the puppies learn resignation—a suitable coping strategy when faced with frustration, and one that will serve them well in dealing with the challenges that life has to offer. Later, as the puppies become more mobile and more persistent, she may fix them with a firm stare, before growling or even snapping toward them to keep them away. This is usually their first experience of canine discipline—and learning to cope with this very dramatic "failure" is also important if they are to become well-balanced adults.

Such early lessons also teach puppies that life is not a "bed of roses." No matter how well cared for, trained, or socialized, dogs always have to deal with challenges, spending time by themselves, or failing to get what they want when they want it. Low-level stress is a fact of life, and needs to be dealt with in a positive way if it is not to affect the individual detrimentally. "Stress immunization" therefore needs to be taken seriously, and care must be taken not to over-protect puppies once they can stand on their own four paws for the majority of the time.

Play also assists in this process. Puppies playing with each other soon learn that they cannot always win every game. Sometimes the resource that they are competing for—such as a toy or a resting space—goes to one individual, sometimes to another. Learning to be a "good loser" means that puppies cope with the stress of failure and accept it, or are forced to work out new strategies that mean they will "win" next time. This is the start of "creativity" in thinking—and can mean the difference between a dog that simply reacts to later training and one that responds with thought, care, and consideration.

Trainers now recognize the fact that dogs can think for themselves. Guide dogs, dogs for the disabled, search and rescue dogs, and drug detection dogs are all perfectly capable of problem-solving in their daily routines—it makes them more flexible in their approach and more adaptable to new environments. In the same way, allowing our own pet dogs to be "creative" in both training and activities will develop our relationships and foster opportunities for dogs to behave in a natural way.

below: *Puppies need to meet and mix with people, other dogs, and other animals well before 12 weeks of age if they are to become well-adjusted adult dogs.*

an objective look at "intelligence"

"Intelligence" is an interesting term. When appreciating canine behavior and cognitive ability, it would be unrealistic to view a dog's intelligence in the same way that we view a human's. Dogs cannot speak a vocal language, and they cannot read or write. However, they can clearly show that they are thinking, sensitive beings if given the opportunity to do so.

Of course, different breeds have different skills and attributes. A retriever may have no problem learning to bring articles back to hand, while a pointer finds locating and indicating shot game relatively easy. However, "intelligence" is also relative in terms of what rewards are offered to the dog. A Border Collie may be considered "intelligent" if it

learns to come back right away when called, but does that make it more intelligent than the Basset Hound that is still sniffing in the undergrowth and having a wonderful time 10 minutes after being called by its owner?

brain games for dogs

exercise one
Hide a small piece of food under an overturned cup. Time how long it takes your dog to knock the cup over to get to the food.
- ■ 1–5 seconds = genius!
- ■ 5–10 seconds = excellent
- ■ 10–30 seconds = could do better
- ■ 30 seconds–2 minutes = he's not hungry!

exercise two
Create an upright barrier, by using furniture or some cardboard. Place the dog's favorite toy on the other side, and then ask it to find the toy. What does it do?
- ■ Rushes around the outside of the barrier to get the toy immediately = genius!
- ■ Jumps over the barrier = excellent
- ■ Sits and looks at you, then paws the barrier = could do better
- ■ Lies down and falls asleep = not in the mood to play games.

exercise three
Place a dog biscuit or small piece of food inside a plastic bottle. Allow him to figure out how to roll it around, shake it, or throw it in order to get the food.

exercise four
Teach your dog a new trick. "Give a paw," "roll over on command," or "play dead" are all tricks that have a useful practical application for handling and grooming, as well as for stretching your dog's brain.

exercise five
Indoors or out, play "hide and seek" the toy, dog biscuit, or person. Ask the dog to sit and wait, then hide the object or person. Count to ten, then send the dog to find it. Give lots of encouragement and praise while it is looking and play a game when

the dog is successful. Gradually make the game more challenging by concealing the object more thoroughly.

exercise six
Utilize your dog's sense of smell and its ability to track by laying simple scent pathways in the yard or out on walks. Choose fresh ground, preferably first thing in the morning, before it has become overrun with other scents.

Lay a short track by simply walking 10–15 paces and place your dog's favorite toy or some food at the end of it. Encourage the dog to follow your track with its nose to get the reward. Gradually extend the length of the track and how complicated it is by walking over rough terrain.

above: *Breed or type characteristics may make some aspects of training, such as retrieving, easier for some dogs.*

opposite page: *Always try to direct your dog's play onto appropriate items—shoes and slippers are not included!*

left: *Keep your dog's mind active with games that help to develop its creativity and allow it to express normal canine behavior in an appropriate way.*

For some dogs that have been trained in a rather "traditional" way, or who have come from a pound or animal shelter, these games may be a little confusing to begin with. If your dog doesn't seem too interested, increase the motivation by offering better rewards. Try not to help out too much—the art of developing problem-solving skills relies on your dog learning to overcome challenges for itself.

above: *Powerful in water, as well as on land.*

left: *The born athlete!*

Form and function: The dog's appearance has been changed dramatically by man over centuries of breeding, but fitness shines through.

the look of a
dog

the **basic** model

Dogs are one of the most diverse species on earth. Their physical appearance, size, and even behavior vary so greatly that it's hard to imagine that they all originate from a single blueprint. In most cases, man has intervened in the natural selection process to create such diversity. We have bred dogs for work—long legs for speed, upright ears for sensitive hearing, or low, long bodies to be able to fit down rabbit holes. Along the way, man also started to breed for looks—long, flowing coats, color, and head shape have all come under scrutiny, and the belief that dogs are creatures of aesthetic beauty, as well as workers or companions, has developed.

In a few areas of the world, domestic dogs have had the opportunity to breed freely, without the interference of man. Some have even reverted to living a wild existence—learning to hunt as a

left: *Straight bones, a balanced body, and an alert expression: this puppy is raring to go!*

above: *A long, flowing coat will need extra care.*

team once again and scavenging to eke out an existence.

The dingoes of Australia are probably the best-known group of semi-wild dogs today. Living completely without human help, they have flourished in hot, arid

below: *The ultimate "urban dingo"?*

countryside where other animals have failed to survive, and have raised generations of pups in the harshest of conditions. Interestingly, these dogs have also reverted to "type."

Dingoes are characterized by their sandy-colored short coats, which reduce the effect of the intense heat of the sun, but also offer enough insulation to maintain body warmth at night. They are large and powerful, but without any excess of skin or bone that might hinder hunting. Long legs provide speed for chasing, while a long, narrow muzzle houses a formidable set of teeth, ideal for killing prey. Dingoes are also highly social. In order to successfully raise puppies, they need to work together to provide food and shelter for the whole pack—and their communication systems are advanced enough to make this effective.

While groups of feral dogs, such as the dingoes, are rare, perhaps this "basic model" of a dog tells us something about the "ultimate" dog shape and construction. Despite the lack of prepared pet food, central heating, or advanced veterinary care, dingoes seem to flourish, because they are built to do so.

Looking at an average pet dog is a slightly different matter, simply because so many have a strong pedigree influence—but wander around any animal shelter and a similar phenomenon can be seen.

Left to breed naturally—dogs of different types mating either by design or accident—many crossbreeds or mongrels seem to take on a similar appearance. Few "urban dingoes" have to contend with the heat of the desert, so their coats are rarely sandy colored. Instead, they are often darker shades, even black. They are medium in size and usually have short, harsh coats. While the influences of certain breeds, such as upright German Shepherd-type ears, or Labrador otter-tails, can often be seen in their outward appearance, they are often perfectly designed to adapt to an urban environment.

Such "urban dingoes" nearly always make great pets. While they may lack the exotic good looks or grace of some of the pedigree breeds, they are often healthy and hardy, easy to train, affectionate, and eminently adaptable to all kinds of urban living.

appearance with a purpose

The basic model is powerfully built, although housed in a compact frame. Flexible and athletic, the dog is able to extend its muscles sufficiently to make running, jumping, and turning at high speeds almost effortless.

The front legs are straight and strong, for pouncing and digging. The head is fairly broad, with a narrow muzzle. Dark eyes are highlighted by expressive eyebrows and lashes. Mobile ears allow sounds to be gathered and focused. A relatively long tail, broad at the base and tapering to the tip, is mobile in all directions to facilitate communication, balance, and direction while swimming.

body sizes and shapes

Body shapes and sizes in dogs are nearly always a reflection of their original roles. In breeding certain types of dog for particular jobs, man would have selected those that showed special skills or abilities and mated them to others with the same qualities. In this way it is possible to define body shapes and sizes.

sprinters

Sprinters are, obviously, built for speed. They are usually able to cover short distances very rapidly, but do not have a great deal of stamina. The Greyhound is probably the best known of this type of dog. Lean and muscular, the dog is very narrow to reduce wind resistance and has a huge lung capacity, which needs to be housed in a deep chest. Limb extension is important, to

below: *Built for speed, not strength, sprinters can reach speeds of 37 mph (60 km/h).*

ensure as much ground is covered in a single stride as possible. Such dogs are surprisingly tall—Afghan Hounds and Borzois, which are also in this category, stand about 29–31 inches (73–79 cm) at the shoulder. This makes hunting by sight easier, as the horizon can be scanned for small animals and prey that may be moving.

long-distance runners

Dogs that are able to travel long distances are quite different in shape from those that run fast in short bursts. Endurance runners tend to pace as opposed to gallop or sprint—and so require less extension from the shoulder joint. This usually makes them more compact in height and depth. Lung capacity still needs to be good, so the dog's chest is moderately deep, but more space is given to muscle and stored fat. The dog needs sustenance along the way and will use up its own reserves if

above: *The ultimate "ratter"— a Jack Russell Terrier.*

food is not immediately forthcoming.

Many of the dogs that have been bred as excellent cross-country endurance runners are arctic breeds. Sled dogs have been used for thousands of years to transport man across the ice and snow—and for this reason all the huskies, the Malamute, and the Eskimo dog are covered in a thick blanket of hair.

heavyweights

In many cases, the size and stature of the heavy breeds reflects their original function—as fighting dogs or carting dogs. Such breeds as Mastiffs, Bulldogs, Bullmastiffs, Tosas, and Boxers were originally bred to fight bulls, bears, or even other dogs. These dogs needed substance and strength, as well as resilience and endurance. Bones needed to be thick and strong, while the head and neck needed to be powerful and muscular. Speed was not important, so lung capacity or the ability to extend limbs were not a consideration.

Other heavyweight breeds were used to pull loads. Carting breeds, such as the Bernese Mountain Dog or the Rottweiler, needed power and bulk, as well as agility to move weights behind them. The original tug-boat dog, the Newfoundland, needed strength, tenacity, and endurance to move heavy craft through the water and on land.

ground workers

Dogs that are bred to go to ground need to be fast and agile. A terrier permanently stuck in an underground burrow is not likely to pass its genetic material on to the next generation, so they tend to be slim, long-bodied, short-legged dogs, with the ability to turn around in very confined spaces. Such dogs were not usually required to cover a lot of ground by running or

above: *Smart and alert, this toy dog was bred as a companion.*

trotting, so lung capacity was secondary to a streamlined shape.

relay racers

Dogs that run relays, either to retrieve things and bring them back to their owner or to herd animals and bring them back to their owner, need to be well-balanced overall. They are likely to need to compromise between speed and endurance, so they tend to be large dogs with a good chest capacity, but somewhat more substantial than the sprinters. Retrievers and Collies both fall into this middle-distance category, and are often good swimmers, too.

companion dogs

Dogs bred as companions rarely need to run or pace for any great distance. They are usually small enough to lie on their owner's lap and be picked up. Their body shapes and sizes are often miniaturized or neotenized—with large heads and smaller bodies, so that the dog appears to be permanently immature. The Pekingese and Chihuahua spring to mind as good examples of this category.

left: *The heavyweights of the dog world, St. Bernards are huge and powerful.*

skin structure,
coat types, coloring

The skin acts as physical protection against the elements, and helps to maintain the dog's body temperature. In addition to being sensitive to hot or cold, the skin is sensitive to touch and pain.

the structure of the skin

The skin is made up of two main layers—the epidermis and the dermis. The epidermis is the outer layer of cells. This layer replaces itself as the top surface is shed or gets worn away, in exactly the same way as ours does.

Under the epidermis, the next layer—the dermis—is strong and flexible. This layer provides the nerve and blood supply to the epidermis above. Sweat glands open through the epidermis. In dogs these are primarily on the pads of the feet and in the ear canals. Dogs lose very little heat through the hair-covered surface of their bodies; they sweat through their feet and pant.

the coat

Hair follicles emerge through the epidermis. In dogs, a number of hairs emerge from the same opening. One hair is often thicker and longer than the others, and this is called the guard hair. Quite often, this hair is a different color than the ones surrounding it—giving a flecked appearance to the coat. Sebaceous glands feed into the hair follicle to keep the skin lubricated and the coat glossy.

Small muscle fibers in the dermis—the deeper layer of the skin—can control movement of the guard hairs on the surface. By contracting or lengthening these muscles when excited or aggressive, dogs can achieve piloerection, which most of us know as "raising the hackles."

The dog's hair grows in cycles. This means that hair is either being grown, is in a transitional phase, or is in a resting phase. A hair is only shed, or molted, when a new one is ready to replace it. The length of time this takes is dependent on the weather, the number of daylight hours, and the dog's hormones. Dogs normally shed hair when they least need it—in the spring and fall. However, the effects of central heating can influence this natural body clock and result in shedding at other times.

top: *Immense wrinkling around the face and eyes characterizes the Shar Pei.*

left: *Aptly named, the Mexican Hairless dog is completely bald.*

types of coat

The length and type of the dog's coat is genetically determined. Some breeds have a thick undercoat, which is usually softer and lighter than the harsher outercoat. This traps air and acts as efficient insulation against the cold. This is usually the coat that falls out while shedding. Other breeds, such as Labradors, have very little undercoat, but have very close, sometimes harsh hair that acts as a waterproof layer, repelling water from the surface.

Coats can be straight and fine, such as the Weimaraner's, or dense and curly, such as the Poodle's. In a few rare breeds, such as the Puli and Komondor,

above: *Known throughout the world, the Afghan Hound is famous for its flowing coat.*

the coat is designed to form into mats, trapping natural oils and increasing water and cold resistance.

color

The wide variety of colors of dog hair means that a whole set of definitions has grown up. Brown is not just brown—it may be "chocolate" or "liver." Gray hues are usually "blue," while a black-and-white Great Dane is properly described as a "harlequin."

Particolor: markings in two colors, such as black and tan or black and white.

Tricolor: markings in three colors, such as black, white, and tan.

Wheaten: a golden color.

Sable: predominantly gray, fawn, silver, or gold, but each hair has a black tip.

Roan: a mix of white and colored hair —usually "orange" or "blue."

Brindle: tiger stripes of black hairs on a lighter background color.

right: *The "Silver Shadow" of the dog world: a beautiful Weimaraner.*

left: *The Hungarian Viszla is a distinctive russet gold color.*

61

head shapes and sizes

Looking at the profile of a breed such as a St. Bernard, and comparing it to that of a Chihuahua, it is hard to believe that these two creatures belong to the same species. The massive head of the St. Bernard, with its square brow and broad, square muzzle, is in complete contrast to that of the tiny rounded dome of the toy dog. How can such diversity be explained?

One theory is that as different breeds and types of dog evolved to do specific tasks, so their head shapes began to alter. The wolf has a very distinct head shape. Broad across the forehead, with wide-set eyes for good peripheral vision, the muzzle is long and square, for maximum impact. Diversifying from this basic format, domestic dogs now show characteristics that fall into three distinct groups of head shape.

Dolichocephalic, or long-nosed breeds, tend to have narrow heads and muzzles. Many of the dogs in this group are long and lean in body shape too—Greyhounds, Salukis, and Borzois are all good examples.

Mesocephalic head shapes are more rounded than the original blueprint of the wolf's—with a shorter, squarer muzzle, although this is without exaggeration. The retrievers and pointers fall into this category.

Brachycephalic breeds, such as Boxers, Pugs, and Bulldogs, have the most extreme head shapes, with very broad skulls and very short noses. Some of the dogs in this category, such as the Pekingese, have lost the muzzle altogether.

All three of these categories reflect the work that such breeds were bred to do. The slender head of the dolichocephalic breeds reduces air resistance and allows for a wide field of vision. The strong muzzles of the mesocephalic breeds reflects their ability to carry game or other prey, while the brachycephalic breeds often stem from dogs used for fighting—the Boxer's nose, for example, was designed

above: *A Pekingese puppy.*

below: *The Bloodhound shows huge ears.*

to allow the dog to hang onto the end of a bull's nose and still breathe freely.

Today, it is rare for the majority of pet dogs to work, but we have retained or even emphasized their head shapes. Some theories attribute physical and behavioral anomalies, such as breathing problems, aggression, and anxiety to the breeding of dogs for appearance alone.

the skull

Although the skull shapes of different breeds vary greatly, they all contain the same bones. Each skull forms a box shape, called the cranium. The upper jaw is made up of the maxilla bone, while the lower jaw is hinged to the skull by the mandibles.

Just as in human development, the bony plates that make up the top of the skull fuse together in the middle of the forehead. In a few breeds, such as Chihuahuas, which have very domed heads, the fusion fails, leaving a gap or fontanelle. This can have implications for life-long injury to the brain.

eye positions

The way the eyes are set into the dog's skull influences not only its appearance, but also its range of vision. The dog has a wide field of vision in comparison to a human; we can claim a 100° field of vision. Flat-nosed breeds, such as the Pug, are likely to have a 200° field of vision, whereas sight-hounds, such as the Afghan Hound or Borzoi, have a 270° field of vision. This helps them to scan large areas, looking for prey or movement.

different nose shapes

The dog's nose contains vast numbers of sensory cells. These are located in the olfactory membrane. The size of a dog's nose can therefore indicate whether it was bred to work by

above: *A wolf in Labrador clothing!*

following scent, or whether another sense, such as sight, is more important to its work. For example, it is estimated that a Dachshund's nose contains 125 million sensory cells, while a German Shepherd may have up to 220 million. A human is thought to have around five million.

below: *Erect ears and "wolf-like" facial markings reveal the Husky's origins.*

ear shapes and sizes

Variation in ear size and shape among dogs is vast, but the external shape of the ear does not seem to influence the functioning of the inner ear or the dog's hearing in any way. However, the shape and mobility of the ear affects the dog's ability to gather sounds and focus on them, as well as their use as a signaling tool in communication. This may explain why the dog's ancestor, the wolf, has large, fully upright ears, which can swivel from side to side and also flatten backward. The wolf's ears have 17 muscles to support and move them, independently and together—making them one of the most expressive and obvious components of body language.

Some breeds, such as the German Shepherd, still have upright ears like the wolf's, which are mobile and expressive. Other breeds, such as the spaniels, have heavy, pendulous ears that couldn't be further from the original design.

A few breeds of dog, such as Poodles, grow hair right inside the ear canal. This can cause dirt and wax to accumulate, and is a breeding ground for bacterial infection. This hair needs to be plucked out on a regular basis to prevent such problems. Once familiarized with the experience, most dogs do not find it uncomfortable.

A dog's ears are one of its most useful communication tools. Dogs show excitement, or sometimes confidence, by making their ears as large and upright as possible. This not only allows them to gather as much auditory information as they can about a situation, but also emphasizes the size of their head—creating a visual signal for other dogs to "read." In fearful situations, or when a dog is

below: *The most famous pendulous ears of all— the Basset Hound.*

64

button ears

These fold over, such as in the Fox Terrier. Such a design may protect the inner ear from dirt and damage.

bat ears

Bat ears are usually large and erect, such as in the French Bulldog. Mobility in these upright ears varies from breed to breed.

butterfly ears

These resemble a butterfly, as the name suggests. The Papillon has beautiful butterfly ears. Long feathering covers the exterior.

drop ears

Drop ears fall flat to the sides of the head or cheeks. The size of the outer ear is dependent on selective breeding.

erect ears

The German Shepherd, Bull Terrier, and Elkhound all have erect ears, although size and positioning may differ from breed to breed.

rose ears

Rose ears are those that expose the smooth inner portion of the ear. Bulldogs and Whippets have rose ears.

showing anxiety, it may flatten its ears to its head—making itself look as small and non-threatening as possible.

ear cropping

In some countries, ear cropping is still practiced. This involves the surgical removal of a part of the ear flap to artificially create a permanently upright ear. Although distasteful, it is widespread in countries where it is legal, and is routinely performed on several breeds including the Doberman, Great Dane, and Boxer.

right: *A Papillon, showing well-feathered "butterfly" ears.*

below: *An American Cocker Spaniel, showing a heavy coat on ears and legs.*

tails

For many dogs, their tail is their pride and joy. The base of the tail is an extension of the spine and, as such, acts as a rudder, a balancing aid, and an emotional barometer.

Tails can be long or short. A few breeds are born without a tail, and some breeders have utilized this genetic feature to alter the construction of other breeds that are normally docked.

Most dogs have very mobile tails. Their movement is primarily from side to side, in order to be able to wag, although vertical movements are important, too. Some breeds, such as many of the spitz types, carry their tails curled right up and over the back when aroused or excited. However, for most dogs, holding the tail high is designed to indicate confidence, or even dominance.

Dogs tails are thought to wag for a variety of reasons. The main reason is to indicate intention and mood. Emotion can be shown by the position in which the tail is held, the width of the tail wag itself, and the frequency of the wag. A wagging tail does not always mean happiness or friendliness. Dogs wag their tails in a low position to indicate uncertainty or even fear, and a tail that is tucked underneath the dog's body, yet is still wagging, is clearly not indicating pleasure or confidence.

It is possible that tail wagging helps

above: *The long, feathered tail of a Cardigan Corgi.*
below: *Tails show mood and intention, in this case anxiety.*

to spread scent signals for other dogs' information. Scent is produced from the anal sacs and also from urine, and a wagging tail may waft these scents to distribute them.

Under the dog's tail lies the anus, through which the anal sacs are expressed. These two sacs lie at either side of the anus, at roughly the "ten-to-two" position on a clock face. They contain a mixture of substances, which carry olfactory information for other

left: *A Rottweiler with a closely docked tail, traditional in the breed.*

dogs and which get deposited with fecal matter.

Occasionally, a dog's anal sacs may become blocked or infected. If this happens, the dog may bite frantically at the base of his tail, or may "scoot" his bottom along the ground to rub the affected area. If this occurs, it is likely that the anal sacs need to be expressed manually—by squeezing in exactly the right spot and catching the resulting discharge in cotton batting or tissues. Your veterinarian will show you how to perform this simple procedure. One word of warning, however: anal sac secretions smell foul. Indeed, some dogs will express them if they feel threatened in some way—presumably to put the adversary off with the offensive smell.

Tail docking used to be commonplace in many countries. This involves the removal of the whole tail or a part of it when the puppy is under a week old, usually by cutting it off, or by restricting blood flow to the tail by the use of a very tight elastic band. It is now illegal for any person other than a veterinarian to perform tail docking in many countries, although the majority of puppies from traditionally docked

breeds are still being docked.

The arguments for docking are that working dogs can sustain tail injuries when in the field. However, the vast majority of dogs now bred in the United States and Europe are pet dogs. Those that do work are usually assisted by the tail, not hindered by it, as it helps to steer the dog when

swimming, can aid balance when running or jumping, and signals behavioral intention to other dogs.

above: *A Border Collie shows how the tail is used for balance when moving.*

below: *Raised slightly higher than its back, this German Shepherd's tail shows excitement and anticipation.*

the pet
dog

above: *Friends for life.*

left: *Happy family!*

Owning a dog can be the greatest joy or the worst nightmare. With time, thought, and commitment, a dog can offer affection, companionship, the opportunity to get more exercise and meet people, and even the chance to compete in a new sport. However, dogs can also be time-consuming, a tie to the home, and even a liability to yourself and others.

deciding to get a dog

Research suggests that dogs can be beneficial to human health. Dog owners are proven to suffer from fewer colds and other minor illnesses, are less likely to be depressed or lonely, and can even enjoy the benefits of lowered blood pressure after stroking a friendly pet. However, all these benefits can be reversed in one fell swoop if the dog is untrained, unsociable, or aggressive—the end result is up to you.

Time is at a premium for most people in our busy world, and space is becoming more and more limited. Society now places more restrictions on pets and pet owners than ever before. Dogs cannot be taken into many stores or parks, are even completely banned in some cities of the world, and their behavior is constantly under scrutiny.

Even normal canine behavior, such as barking or going to the bathroom has to be carefully controlled or owners may contravene local laws.

Such restrictions mean that dogs have to be more thoroughly trained, more controlled when out in public, and have to compete for their owner's time and energy. Before even getting a dog, prospective owners should think about why they want a dog, and whether they really have the time, money, and energy to make the commitment to owning this wonderful and companionable animal.

Dogs need companionship. They cannot be left at home all day by

top: *Devotion and assistance.*

left: *Dogs can provide companionship and the incentive for regular exercise—but are also a responsibility.*

themselves without suffering some degree of distress. Dogs also need to be taken care of if you go away for the weekend or on vacation, so kenneling or the dog-sitter's fees need to be taken into consideration. Food and veterinary bills will need to be taken care of, and although many pet insurance companies offer excellent coverage for emergency care and for essential third-party insurance, they do not pay for the cost of routine vaccinations or preventive treatments, such as worming.

Quite apart from the expenses involved, all dogs need exercise and training. While the children may be eager to walk the puppy for the first few weeks, the dog will need a walk every day for the rest of its life—come wind, rain, or snow, and this usually falls to the adults in the household.

All dogs need grooming, but some breeds or types have more specific requirements than others, which may mean long hours of brushing or paying for professional grooming on a regular basis. Even breeds with short, low-maintenance hair usually shed—all over the carpet, clothing, and furniture—while muddy paws can create havoc in an immaculately kept home.

All in all, dogs provide a chance for us to nurture a social creature unconditionally, and to receive affection and love in return. However, the cost of such love is not insignificant, either in financial terms or in terms of time. Can you be sure that you will be able to make such a commitment for the next 15 years? If not, be strong-minded and review your situation again in a few months' time. Good things in life are always worth waiting for.

above: *Contrary to popular belief, dogs and cats can become good friends.*

below: *All dogs need exercise and mental stimulation. Can you afford the time?*

choices of dog

Choosing a dog can be an exciting but confusing task. Not only do you need to choose a breed or type that suits your needs and lifestyle, you need to decide whether or not to pick a puppy or an adult, a male or a female.

pedigree or crossbreed?

There are some major advantages to buying a pedigree dog. The first of these is that you will be able to predict the size, shape, and, to a certain degree, the behavioral characteristics of the dog as an adult (*see box*). This means that if you are considering a West Highland White Terrier, for example, you can predict that it will be small, white, and possess terrier drives—he or she may enjoy barking, will like to dig, and may be feisty with other dogs, but is also likely to be lively, affectionate, and responsive if trained and socialized from an early age.

By definition, pedigree dogs share the same ancestry, and this means that they are also likely to share the same physiological defects. Nearly all pedigree breeds are known to have some hereditary defects—hip dysplasia, eye problems, or heart abnormalities are among them. However, a responsible breeder will have tested all breeding stock for known problems,

above: *All puppies are irresistible, but be sure their parents are clear of hereditary problems.*

and should only breed from clear parents to produce offspring that are least likely to inherit defects.

The lack of such hereditary problems in crossbreeds and mixed breeds is one reason why choosing a non-pedigree can be attractive. Certainly, crossbreeds (where each parent is of a different known breed) and mongrels (where the parentage is totally mixed through past generations) are often thought to have "hybrid vigor"—although this does not prevent them from contracting disease and having clinical problems like any other dog.

It may be difficult to tell how large a crossbreed puppy will eventually become—or what behavioral characteristics it will have inherited from its mother and father. However, the size of the paws and the length of the hocks may give a clue to eventual size.

puppy or adult?

A puppy can be molded, trained, and socialized to fit your life and environment, but this takes a lot of time, commitment, and work. Although adult dogs are usually very adaptable,

left: *Mixed breeds are less likely to suffer from hereditary diseases, but their eventual size and behavior can be less predictable.*

it is possible that you will be inheriting someone else's rearing and training—even their problems. However, adult dogs are often housebroken, cutting down on the need for training in the early stages, and many are worldly wise, having already learned about children, traveling, and a domestic environment. Many dogs needing new homes are merely victims of circumstance—the casualties of their previous owners' house moves, career changes, or marriage break-ups—and they deserve a second chance.

male or female?

Much speculation surrounds this question. Certainly, for most breeds or types, bitches tend to be easier to train and are more biddable. However, they do come into season twice a year. This can be prevented entirely by early neutering, and most vets in the United States recommend that a bitch be neutered prior to her first heat.

Males may be more inclined to aggression toward other dogs outside the home, and although this can often be minimized by neutering, too, they may require extra socialization and training.

top: *Bitches are generally easier to train than males, but don't forget that they come into season twice a year....*

left: *Puppies are cute, but think what kind of care your adult dog will need.*

different breeds have different needs

If you are thinking about buying a pedigree dog, choose carefully, bearing in mind the type to which that breed belongs. All pedigree dogs have been bred to do a job—and this will influence their appearance and behavior to some extent.

working breeds

This group includes all the herding dogs—which will often herd children, joggers, and cyclists in the absence of sheep. Considerable training and mental stimulation are usually required.

gundogs

Often like to hold things in their mouths. Usually need above-average amounts of exercise. May be scatterbrained and highly active as youngsters.

terriers

Fast responses and sometimes reactive. Males can be aggressive toward other dogs if not socialized extensively when young.

toy dogs

May be reactive with children. Usually highly dependent on their owners, and affectionate.

utility breeds

This group includes dogs bred for unique purposes. Research the breed and look at its original task—then think about how the dog may express such behaviors in a modern human society. Many require substantial exercise and very early socialization with other dogs.

where to get a dog

Serious consideration needs to be given to the question of where to obtain your dog. Buying from an inappropriate source can make or break the entire experience. Sadly, there are now far too many outlets for unscrupulous breeders who breed dogs purely for profit, without any consideration for their health, behavior, or future welfare.

In many countries puppy farms exist legally—where large numbers of puppies of all kinds and breeds are produced *en masse*, to be distributed and sold. While some of these pups may be unharmed by the experiences of their early weeks, others are kept in squalid conditions removed from their

above: *Many, many dogs are in animal shelters, awaiting new homes. Choosing an adult dog that suits you takes time and care.*

left: *Grooming helps to establish a trusting relationship, as well as to maintain good health.*

mothers and littermates too soon, and have to travel long distances to be sold from outlets, such as pet stores, in different geographical regions.

These puppies may have long-term physical problems, hereditary defects, and the potential for behavioral problems. For this reason, it is always a good idea to see a puppy with its mother and the rest of its litter in the place where it was born. Ideally, see the father, too—this will give you an idea of the combination of characteristics that your pup will have inherited from both dam and sire—although in many cases the stud dog lives a long distance away, so this is simply not possible.

Puppies should be raised in a domestic environment, where they are surrounded by people. The first few weeks of life are vital to your pup's behavioral well-being, and environmental deprivation has far-reaching effects. Research has shown that pups develop mental capacity very quickly—by four weeks of age they are able to process information and learn about the world around them. The time between four and 12 weeks of age is known as the "critical socialization period." This is the time when puppies learn how to cope with the world around them, how to relate to other dogs, and that human contact is desirable.

Ideally, puppies should be born in the center of a family household and stay there until they are ready to go to new homes. This way they become familiar with household noises, smells, and sights long before leaving Mom. Puppies born and raised in a barn, in kennels at the back of the yard, or as one of many litters being raised at the same time, are already at a disadvantage. It is little wonder that dogs are nervous or anxious when meeting new people if they have only seen a human being twice a day, at feeding times.

Good breeders allow you to view and handle the puppies as many times as you want before you decide to take one home. They ask you as many questions as you ask them—such as how many hours a day you are at work and whether your yard is safe. If the only question the breeder asks you is "How would you like to pay?" walk away! And do not buy a puppy if the mother appears to be nervous or aggressive. It is not normal maternal behavior to be aggressive around puppies—and such traits are easily passed on to the next generation.

Finally, try to be strong-minded. It is almost impossible to deny children a puppy once they have seen one, so visit without the kids initially if you are not sure. Do not be pressured into buying a puppy if you have any doubts at all, and certainly do not be lured into buying two pups from the same litter—even if it means leaving one by itself. Two puppies together are nearly always double the trouble, not double the joy.

below: *These Poodles will grow to need considerable time and effort in coat care.*

picking your dog

For the prospective first-time dog owner, the decision to buy an adult dog or a puppy is an important one, not only for the human but also for the future welfare of the animal.

choosing a puppy

For many people, their actual choice of puppy is limited—because they specifically want a bitch or a dog, or a certain color or length of coat. However, if this is not the case, being faced with a whole litter of pups and trying to choose one can be daunting.

Obviously, picking a puppy that is in perfect health is the priority. A puppy should have bright, clear eyes, clean ears with no discharge or smell, and a shiny, healthy coat with no signs of fleas or mites. It should feel plump, but have no distention of the stomach—which may indicate the presence of worms—and should be clean around the tail.

Obviously, puppies need to sleep a great deal, and if you happen to visit the pups while they are resting, they may not appear very bright or active.

If this occurs, waiting until the pups are awake, or returning to visit at another time, is essential—you need to be able to see that all the puppies are alert, curious, and mobile before buying. Any puppy that sits still in the corner, lies quietly while all the others are bouncing around, or is hunched while moving may be unwell. Do not be swayed if the breeder says that the pups have just been wormed, or have had upset

below: *Handle your pup all over.*

above: *Staff members at most animal shelters are happy to help you make a sensible selection.*

right: *Cute and appealing—but will he suit your lifestyle?*

stomachs when explaining any signs of sickness or weight loss—be strong-minded and arrange to see them again rather than regret the decision later.

Assuming that all the puppies are bright-eyed and active, the pups' behavior is the next consideration. Nearly every litter of pups contains some that are bold and confident, even a little pushy, as well as one or two that are more reserved, even a little anxious. In between are the average puppies—normal, well-balanced, curious, and confident, but not too demanding in their behavior—these usually make the best pets.

Bearing this in mind, it is perhaps best to avoid choosing the puppy that chooses you. Unless you intend to work this dog, or are an experienced trainer, this puppy may well be a little too confident for you. Similarly, you should avoid the puppy that sits at the back, quivering at the sight of new faces, sights, and smells—a nervous

individual needs double the socialization and care to ensure that it becomes a confident pet.

choosing an adult dog

Selecting an adult dog from an animal shelter can be even more difficult than choosing a puppy. All those sad faces looking at you through the bars of kennel doors are enough to melt even the strongest will. Try to bear in mind what kind of dog will suit your lifestyle and space—and pick on the basis of behavior, size, activity level,

and grooming requirements, rather than appearance. Sometimes the least attractive dog in a kennel can make the best pet if given the chance for a new home.

Try to get as much information about the dogs as possible before choosing. Although many dogs come into shelters as strays, and therefore have no known history, there may be some background details about others, and kennel staff are often able to give a character profile of a dog's behavior since it arrived at the kennel.

your **new** dog's
basic needs

Just like humans, dogs have several basic needs—water, food, shelter, and a suitable place in which to relieve themselves. Very few people would be able to live a fulfilled and contented life with just these bare necessities, and dogs are no different. They are a social species, and as such they need companionship, security, play, and lessons in how to behave socially.

In order to build the best possible relationship with your dog, it is vital to address both its basic physical needs, and its emotional ones, too.

basic essentials

Water: A fresh supply of drinking water should be constantly available to your dog. Dogs drink varying amounts, depending on a number of different factors: what kind of food they are eating, the temperature, and how well and fit they are generally. In fact, a sudden or dramatic increase in the amount of water that your dog drinks can be an indication that there is a clinical problem that needs investigation by a vet.

Food: It is always wise to bring home or buy exactly the same kind of food that your dog has been used to eating, either in the pound or shelter or in its

above: *Moist, semi-moist, and dry foods are all available—but check their ingredients before feeding.*

last home. Serving the same food for a few days helps to ease the dog's stress at being in a new environment. Changing diet may upset its digestive system if not done very carefully and gradually. Once the dog is settled, you can change its food if you want to, or if you think that it might benefit from a change (*see box opposite*).

There are now hundreds of different kinds of pet food on the market. Each one claims to be the best for your dog, but how can you be sure? The key to knowing what you are really feeding your pet is to look carefully at the label on the food and interpret the information given.

• Look at the label on the food. Is the food **complete**—so that it can be fed to the dog without anything else being added—or **complementary**,

so that another element, such as bread or meat needs to be added to the food to provide a balanced diet?

• Look at the ingredients list. A good, pure source of protein should be in the first two or three ingredients listed. If the food contains "meat and animal derivatives" or "cereals," you cannot tell what is really in the food. Chicken, poultry, egg, lamb, or turkey are all excellent and easily digested sources of protein.

• Is the food described as being for the average pet dog? Feeding a diet designed for "active" or "working" dogs, often called "performance," "field," or "premium," to an average pet dog could result in overactivity and excess energy.

above: *A tasty "extra"—dog biscuits can help to keep teeth healthy.*

left: *Dog dishes come in all shapes and sizes.*

Is your dog's diet really suitable?

A number of different traits may indicate that your dog's diet is not ideal. If those listed below look familiar, it may be worth gradually changing your dog's food to a different brand or type.

- Eating unusual items, such as tissues, sticks, grass, or other fibers, such as those found in wood, wallpaper, even clothing.
- Eating large amounts, yet never gaining weight.
- Bad breath or flatulence.
- Inconsistent stools—sometimes loose stools, sometimes constipated.
- Lack of concentration or attention.
- Overactivity, even after exercise.
- Irritations or allergic reactions to external factors such as fleas or grass.
- Smelly, frequent, large bowel movements.
- Eating own feces.
- Rubbing, chewing, or scratching at the feet, stomach, or base of the tail.

- Although it was traditional to feed a family dog just once a day, modern thought now encourages owners to split the food into two meals. Will the food be easy to split like this?

In recent years, more emphasis has been placed on healthy eating for humans, and this trend is being extended to pets. There are some claims that added colorants or preservatives may have a long-term impact on health, and that some foods may exacerbate, or even cause, behavior problems. Protein types and levels have also come under fire, and it is certainly worth discussing diet with a behavior specialist or your vet if you are worried.

resting places

All dogs need a place of their own in which to sleep, or just to get away from the children or other animals. This could be a basket, an indoor kennel (sometimes called a crate), or just a blanket on the floor, but it needs to be positioned away from the center of activity. Encourage your dog to go there by making it comfortable. Never send your dog there as a punishment or it may start to associate the place with your anger.

below: *Home, sweet home—every dog needs a corner it can call its own.*

emotional and psychological needs

Dogs are social beings—they come from a long line of social ancestors that lived in packs and worked and played together. Indeed, an individual in a wild pack of dogs is unlikely to be alone from the moment it is born to the moment it dies—yet we expect domestic dogs to cope with long periods of separation.

Dogs need a great deal of human contact and companionship. They need to play, to strengthen the bond and relationship between themselves and family members, and they need considerable training in order to learn what humans find socially acceptable.

Dogs are not born understanding human values or knowing the meaning of the words we use. Each and every tiny detail of the way in which we live with them needs to be learned—and the responsibility is ours to teach them in a gentle and sensitive way.

Of course, it would be unrealistic to expect a dog to be with his owner for 24 hours a day. All dogs should be taught how to cope with being alone for short periods by training in short-and-frequent sessions in the first few weeks of being in a new home. Puppies, especially, need to learn that

they can play by themselves.

Interactive toys, such as the Kong— a hollow rubber pyramid—and play balls and cubes, are specially designed so that food can be put inside them. As the dog plays with the toy, food comes out, effectively rewarding the dog for playing. Equally important, however, is play with a new owner. Even in hard times, wild dogs and wolves still make time to play with each other. Both adults and children

the rules of the pack and respond well to clear boundaries gently but firmly held in place by all the family from the first day. Dogs do not understand that although they were allowed to jump up to greet visitors when they were small and cuddly, once they are fully grown and have muddy paws they get shouted at. Nor do dogs appreciate that Mom says they must not get on the sofa, while Dad encourages them up to watch television. Preventing behavior problems is far easier than attempting to cure them later on—so set some basic ground rules and stick to them, no matter how appealing those puppy eyes are.

should be encouraged to play with a dog with its toys, and the dog should be taught to give up the toy immediately when asked. This makes the number of games, both indoors and out, almost endless.

social boundaries

Just like children, dogs need emotional security. They learn that they are secure in a number of ways, but first and foremost is consistency. As a social animal, they understand

the **first** day

Bringing your puppy home is a truly exciting experience—and a little nerve-wracking, too. This is likely to be the first time your puppy has been away from his or her mother and littermates—away from a familiar and secure environment—and it is likely to be somewhat bewildering at first. Even an adult dog, coming into a different home from a shelter or different domestic environment, is likely to find new people, surroundings, sights, and smells somewhat overwhelming for the first few hours. There are, however, a number of things you can do to ensure that your puppy or new dog settles in quickly and calmly, without too much anxiety or stress—on either side.

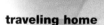

above: *Security, warmth, comfort, and attention will all be required on your puppy's first day. A cozy resting place is essential.*

traveling home

Ideally, your puppy or dog will already have had experience with traveling in a car. If not, you need to bear in mind what a strange experience this must be. Try to ensure that someone comes with you to pick up the puppy—someone who can then drive while the other holds the pup securely on the back seat. If not, then a crate, or traveling cage, can be a useful alternative for keeping your puppy contained while you drive.

Like young children, young dogs are carsick to begin with—so a plentiful supply of paper towels or old towels is a sensible idea. Try to keep the puppy as still and as calm as possible. Reassurance is important, but try to praise for quiet behavior, rather than giving attention for crying or whining.

Starting out right is always a good idea—and restraining a young

left: *Safety in the car should be paramount. Dogs need to be secured or be behind a safety grille.*

boisterous dog by using a special dog car harness or a safety grille is also wise.

Once home, your puppy or dog will almost certainly need to go to the bathroom. Although all of the family probably can't wait to meet it, let your dog out into the backyard and offer gentle praise if there are results. If not, bring the dog indoors, but be aware that it will probably need to go in a little while. Try not to allow a puppy to become overwhelmed by too much attention on the first day. It will need to explore the house, find its water bowl and bed area, and have the opportunity to look around without

too many hands touching or trying to pick it up.

Adult dogs also need a chance to explore—although if you want to restrict their movements around the house, it is wise to block access to certain rooms from the start. A baby gate or stair gate can work wonders for this.

Most puppies that have been raised in a domestic environment are extremely adaptable—and soon figure out that the decor and layout of their new home may be different, but the general structure is the same. After a period of adventuring, most puppies

become tired and flop down to sleep. This is a great opportunity to carefully pick up your puppy and place it in the room or area that you want it to sleep in at night. This might be a crate or basket, or even a cardboard box with a blanket inside. If you have picked up your puppy in the morning, this strategy allows a number of opportunities to familiarize the puppy with the idea of sleeping by itself while napping for short periods and waking up without littermates, before nighttime comes and it is expected to cope for a full eight hours.

Don't forget that as soon as your puppy wakes up, he will need to go outside to relieve himself. This is the start of effective housebreaking.

left: *Give your new pup time to meet and greet the family.*

the **first** week

First introductions are always important, and it is natural that you will want your puppy to fit into the family as easily as possible. The first lesson with a new puppy should be to ensure that you can handle it, without any fear on either side. For many dogs, being closely restrained by being picked up or held is an alien and frightening experience. To a dog, being held tightly may indicate that it is under threat and in danger—or is being mounted.

holding a puppy

Place one hand around the pup's chest and support its weight with the other hand under the bottom. Bring the puppy in close to your chest to give it security. Never lift a puppy under the armpits or hold it in mid-air, and always be cautious how you place it back down—puppies often try to jump at the last minute so keep a firm, reassuring grip until you can feel that its full weight is on the floor.

left: *Even if your puppy is too young to go for a real walk, carrying it helps to maintain socialization.*

above: *Allow the pup to roam freely around its domain to ensure that he becomes acclimated to all the sights, smells, and sounds of the household.*

lifting an adult dog

Adult dogs often make unpleasant associations with being lifted—so caution is required. It is normally sensible to use the "calf lift" when picking up an adult dog. With the dog standing sideways, place both arms around its body and legs and scoop it up, gently, in one movement. This technique prevents the dog from attempting to struggle.

first introductions

Ideally, all first introductions to people, children, or other pets should be calm and quiet. The more noise and excitement others make, the more excited the puppy will get and this can set the stage for all future greetings.

children

Most puppies love children, even if they do regard them simply as other puppies. Try to discourage children from picking up the puppy, or crowding it too much. Puppies can get irritable if they are tired or feel anxious, just like toddlers, but instead of crying to show their displeasure, they may struggle to get away or even snap. Stroking gently and giving treats is the ideal way for a child to interact with the puppy at these first meetings.

another dog at home

If you have another dog at home it is always a good idea to let the two dogs meet on neutral territory, on the leash. Ideally, take your adult dog with you to the breeder's to pick up the puppy. Once the two dogs have traveled home together, allow them to get to know each other in the yard. Give the adult dog all your attention—to reassure it that it is still top dog, and pick up any toys or bones that your adult dog might feel the need to defend.

cats

Contrary to the comic-strip image, cats and dogs can be bosom buddies. However, allowing your new dog or puppy to experience the thrill of the chase should be avoided at all costs, as this will reduce your cat's trust and create anxiety. If your cat is bold and confident with dogs, the chance is it will train the puppy very effectively. However, if your cat is not so

confident, following these steps for their first meeting may help:

- If you are using an indoor kennel, or crate, put the puppy inside and close the door. Bring the cat into the room, and allow it to move around at will.
- Next, hold your puppy on a leash in order to restrain it. Cats should always have an escape route or high place they can run to. Distract the puppy with a toy or some food.

above: *Puppies can be taught to regard all kinds of animals as part of their pack. Even rabbits and guinea pigs can be accepted.*

- Repeat these controlled introductions as often as possible. In the meantime it is important that your cat can eat and sleep in peace and that your puppy is prevented from ambushing the cat while it is compromised on the litter box.

other pets

Puppies can be taught to regard many other kinds of pets, such as rabbits, hamsters, and guinea pigs, as part of the family in the same way. Careful introductions and frequent, calm meetings are essential.

above: *Early exposure to confident cats is an essential part of puppy education.*

If you have an older dog that is not yet housebroken, exactly the same methods can be used.

Errorless learning means preventing your puppy from going to the bathroom in the wrong place. If it always goes in the right place you will be able to praise and reward, which speeds learning even more.

Some owners decide to use newspaper in the early stages. However, this approach is harder work in the long term, as you need to housebreak your puppy twice—once

housebreaking

One of your prime considerations during the first week of having your new puppy is housebreaking. Just like human toddlers, some puppies learn to have control over their bodily functions sooner than others, so patience and understanding is required. However, by using an approach called errorless learning, puppies quickly learn what is expected of them and the whole experience remains stress-free.

left: *Be aware of your dog's needs: exercise, play, and training are among them.*

supervise constantly. If you cannot supervise it, either put the puppy in a crate or playpen, or in an enclosed area where you do not mind if there is an accident—such as the kitchen. Then, take it out every 15 minutes if you can, until you have success.

Try not to be angry with your puppy—even if you have caught it in the act of going to the bathroom in the wrong place. Say "outside" in an urgent voice, then take it quickly outside to show it the place you do want used. Being angry may mean that the puppy will make an association with going to the bathroom in front of you and punishment—meaning that it is less likely to go outside and more likely to go behind a chair when you are not looking.

Old-fashioned punishments, such as rubbing the dog's nose in its own mess, or smacking the puppy, are totally counter-productive and cruel. They simply teach the puppy to be fearful and have nothing to do with effective learning of a new behavior.

Some puppies seem to want to return to the same place to relieve themselves—particularly if they have been allowed to go there accidentally a number of times and a scent still remains. Any accidents on carpet or fabrics need to be cleaned with a biological detergent. This breaks down the proteins in the urine and removes more of the smell. Allowing the area to dry thoroughly, then placing your puppy's food dish and allowing him to eat there a few times may help.

to paper, then again outdoors.

Follow this four-step program for successful housebreaking.

1. Learn to predict when your puppy will need to go to the bathroom—usually this is after waking up, after playing, after excitement, such as visitors arriving, and right after meals.

2. At each of these times, take your puppy to the same place outside and wait with it—even if it's raining or snowing. Gently repeating a phrase like "here we are" helps your puppy to remember what it's there for. As soon as your puppy starts to sniff around, or circle, praise very gently.

3. Once the puppy has relieved itself, lavish praise and offer a special treat. In between these events it is wise to take your puppy outside about once an hour. Watch closely for signs that it might need to go; circling or sniffing the ground are usually reliable indicators.

4. If you wait outside with your puppy and it does not go to the bathroom, bring it back in and

the **first** months— socialization

Puppies go through several distinct developmental stages. At birth, they seem helpless and inactive, but gradually they start to learn what life as a dog is all about. At four to five weeks, puppies have all the brain capacity of an adult dog—although obviously not the concentration span. From this time until 12 weeks of age, puppies are learning all about life and how to communicate. This is not instinctive behavior, but a window of opportunity to learn that is so vital it is known as the critical period.

To ensure that your puppy is confident and relaxed as an adult, it needs to have as many experiences as possible before the end of the critical period. At this stage, puppies are like sponges—soaking up information about the world around them and learning how to deal with it.

above: *Jaws and paws—these ten-week-old puppies learn through play.*

Deprivation during this period can have long-term and drastic implications. Research has shown that puppies that have not met and mixed with humans and other dogs prior to 12 weeks are more likely to be fearful or aggressive later in life.

Don't wait until your puppy has had all its vaccinations before embarking on a socialization program. Even if your puppy cannot walk in parks or on the street, you should create

left: *Early lessons in competing for food may be vital for wild dogs' survival, but they are less important for domestic animals.*

opportunities to expose it to the big wide world by taking it in the car with you, carrying it if you can, and by taking it to the homes of others, as well as inviting lots of people over.

Enrolling in a good puppy socialization class also helps. Puppy socialization classes are intended to teach you the techniques for training your dog effectively, right from the start, and also to help your puppy meet and play with other dogs of a similar age. The upper age limit for most puppy classes is 16–18 weeks, so don't delay in signing up.

A good class should contain about eight puppies, all under the 18-week limit, and the instructors should be clear about its aims and objectives. Puppies should not be allowed to simply have a free-for-all romp while the owners watch, but should be learning the basics of training, through kind, gentle methods, at the same time they are learning social skills from members of their species.

Puppies need to enjoy themselves at these classes, so any kind of force or shouting is undesirable. Instead, the instructor should be aware that all puppies learn at their own pace and that the goals of each owner are different.

Socialization is so vital that it's worth considering just what kind of experiences your puppy may have to cope with later in life. Dogs come in all different shapes and sizes, so even though your puppy may have met a Labrador, does it think all dogs look and act the same way? Imagine meeting a St. Bernard for the first time!

Puppies also need to meet as many different types of people as possible—people who wear hats, glasses, or walk with a walker, as well as children of all ages. How about livestock, and other animals? Dogs also need to get used to different modes of transportation. Try creating a checklist for yourself and your puppy, in order to achieve as much in those first weeks as possible.

above: *Out and about. Dogs of all breeds need to have as many different life experiences as possible.*

below: *Canine communication is exact and intricate. Here an adult Border Collie uses clear facial expressions with a pup.*

the **first** months—
bite inhibition

For many owners, the fact that their cute bundle of fluff comes complete with sharp teeth is a big surprise. Few owners of puppies realize in advance that puppy biting is perfectly normal—if socially unacceptable—in puppies under four months of age.

Like toddlers, puppies learn about the world by putting things into their mouths and biting down on them. If the object is inanimate, the puppy can bite hard, and the object doesn't react. However, if the puppy bites something living—such as its mother, littermates, or a human—with the same pressure, the chances are that the response will be extremely negative, so the puppy's learning curve will be steep.

right: *Puppies need to learn how to control the intensity of their biting. Adult dogs usually respond with firm but gentle discipline.*

Puppy biting teaches the puppy just how hard it can bite other living beings, and watching puppies play together makes this apparent. Puppies play by biting each other. All this is entirely friendly—unless one of the pups bites the other a little too hard. If this bite hurts, the puppy will give a really loud yelp, and will refuse to play

for a short time—usually only a matter of seconds.

Copying the way that dogs communicate with each other gives us an opportunity to teach our puppies that we also feel pain if they bite. Humans need to communicate that they are hurt when their puppies mouth them, not that they are

angry—which puppies regard as irrational aggression. If your puppy is mouthing you, yelp loudly, or give a shout, then turn away as if to nurse your wounds. The puppy should look a little surprised when this first happens, but do not expect the biting to stop immediately. Gradually, over the next few weeks, the puppy biting should become more and more gentle, until you yelp even at the slightest pressure. Finally, you can show pain if a puppy even puts its teeth on you. The rule is that dogs can never bite humans, even in play—we are too fragile, and biting should cease altogether.

For some puppies, getting any reaction to their mouthing is highly exciting. This is normally attention-related, and seems to occur particularly in households with small children who react by screaming and running away if the puppy starts to bite their clothes. This then means that other family members rush to the rescue and the puppy is rewarded by too much excitement and attention. Distracting the puppy with toys and not letting either dog or child become over-excited will help. Time-outs, with the puppy put in the crate, playpen, or kitchen for a short time, allow things to calm down.

handling

All dogs need to get used to being handled—both by their owner and by other people—and this can tie in well with a socialization program. Handling is essential, as it allows an owner to notice physical changes, to keep control of the dog in an emergency, and to treat any physical problems. This becomes particularly important when a dog is in pain or discomfort, as an area that is sensitive to the touch is even more difficult to examine if the dog is unfamiliar with the procedure.

Handling should be done every day at this stage, then at least once a week for the rest of the dog's life, usually in conjunction with a grooming session.

To teach your puppy to be calm and quiet during handling, it is important to make it a pleasant experience, so talk quietly and touch gently.

1. With your puppy standing, run your hands lightly all over its body.
2. Now examine specific areas—the eyes and ears, the tail, the paws, and the belly.
3. Gently lift each lip in turn, so that you can inspect your puppy's teeth.

right: *Puppies should be gently handled all over at least once a day.*

above: *Puppies need to learn how to meet and greet all kinds of animals—preferably in slow motion!*

Don't forget that your puppy cannot tell you if an area is overly sensitive—it can only wriggle and try to escape, or mouth you to try to get you to stop. If this happens, use a food treat to distract your puppy and immediately give a reward for calm behavior.

the **first** months— house rules

Dogs are social creatures. In a wild state, they live as part of a pack that works as an effective hunting and puppy-rearing unit. Conflict is rare, and although much ritual posturing and communication goes on to ensure that all pack members understand the rules, pack living is harmonious.

Domestic dogs have evolved to be very different creatures from wild dogs or wolves. They live with us, in our homes, and have monopolized our hearts, too. Yet under the surface of the cuddly exterior, some of the drives that keep a wild pack together remain. Dogs, like children, need boundaries and consistency. They are unlikely to challenge rules that are always kept, but may become frustrated or confused if those rules are sometimes permitted to be broken. Dogs regard us as their "pack leaders" and it is sensible to start off in the way you intend to continue to ensure that your dog feels secure.

Dogs do not denote rank structure or leadership by physical force or aggression. Instead, they use subtle signals that they recognize as indicators of rank. Many of these are very useful to us, and we can adapt them to the way we live to ensure that we communicate in a way the dog understands. Not all these social signals need to be enforced all the time, but many are simply useful ways of ensuring that your dog maintains good manners.

social rank

Canine social order is fairly basic. In simple terms, the higher your rank, the more rights and privileges you are afforded. By looking at these rights

left: *Children and puppies can be best friends if basic ground rules about play and handling are established.*

from the dog's point of view, it is possible to see why some dogs learn to work the system and take advantage of their owners.

1. attention

Give attention—and lots of it—when you decide, not when your dog does. Some dogs develop masterly strategies to ensure that their owner walks them, pets them, and feeds them when they choose, not the other way around. Ignoring attention-seeking can be quite difficult, particularly if you have a bright dog, but if you ever wonder why you can't make a telephone call, why your visitors never seem to stay long, or why you can't eat your meal in peace, maybe you should think about this.

2. sleeping

Many people don't mind if their dog sleeps on the bed or gets on the furniture, but think about this from the dog's point of view. Being rewarded in this way day after day is wonderful, until the day a relative comes to stay or the dog's paws are muddy. Suddenly it is not permitted to do these things and conflict can occur. If you are going to let your dog enjoy these home comforts, make sure you can move it with just one quiet command.

3. toys and games

Toys are wonderful training tools—but this works both ways. If you think that your dog is training you to throw the ball or play tug-o'-war whenever it

asks, or if it walks off in the middle of a game to chew a toy alone, think about restructuring your games so you both benefit. Some dogs love to pit their strength against their owner when playing tug-o'-war. If yours is one of these, make sure you teach your dog to let go instantly with one quiet command.

below: *An exhausting day!*

4. walking the dog

Many dogs get rewarded for pulling on the leash by getting to the park twice as fast. Consistent non-rewarding of this behavior, by stopping as soon as there is tension in the leash, will help. Leaders decide which way to walk and how fast, so if your dog views outings

above: *Sharing is an important play strategy!*

to the park as a hunting expedition and would like to drag you out of the front door all the way there, insist on your rules being implemented.

Predictable boundaries are essential if your dog is to feel safe and secure in its position at the bottom of the pack. Dogs are great companions and walking partners. They are also skilled opportunists, so, even if you have a dog from a shelter that previously had a difficult life, start off as you intend to continue.

below: *As soon as your pup has had its vaccinations, leash-walking is a must.*

the first months—training

Thankfully, pet dog training has come a long way in the last ten years or so. The days of "I say, you do" are gone, now that most people understand the way that dogs learn.

The first few weeks of your puppy's life in his new home are extremely formative in terms of training. Sitting, lying down, coming when called, and even much more complicated exercises, such as retrieving and doing tricks, can be easily taught even at eight to 12 weeks of age, as long as the dog's motivation is sufficient.

Training a dog to do what we want, when we want it to, is really about teaching a foreign language. Dogs already know how to sit, lie down, and run around—all we are doing is teaching them that our words for such things can prompt these actions and that rewards will follow.

Just as most humans need the motivation of a salary to go to work every day, so dogs need some kind of reward for learning new behavior. Not many people would work for a pat on the head from the boss and few dogs work for praise alone, particularly in

the early stages of training. For many dogs, particularly puppies, food is the equivalent of a month's salary—it can act as the ultimate reward, and is also useful as a lure in the initial stages of training, too.

However, you don't want to rely on food forever, so the use of a "conditioned reinforcer" is essential. This means that you give the dog a signal that it has done the right thing and that a reward is coming. To build

above: *A clicker. This little tool can improve your communication with an animal quickly and effectively. Find a clicker trainer if you need help.*

this signal you can use a small tool called a clicker, or a single sound, such as "Yes" that you pair with a food reward. Make the sound, then give the pup a food treat. Repeat this several times until the sound makes your pup look around instantly for its reward. You are now ready to begin training.

coming when called

- Stand in front of your dog and call in a friendly voice. "Sam, come!"
- Wiggle a piece of food in your outstretched hand. Start moving backward. Clap your hands or make a noise if your dog ignores you.
- If the dog moves just one step toward you, make the sound that tells the dog it is right: "Yes," or click, then give the food.

left: *The smaller and tastier the food treat used in training, the better.*

- Gradually increase the distance it has to come to get the food. Practice by calling your dog to you at unusual moments in and around the house.

sit

- Hold a food treat close to your dog's nose. Now lift your hand up and back, so the dog has to look straight up. The movement of looking upward means its rump has to go down.
- As soon as your dog's rear hits the ground, give the signal and then the treat.
- Add the word "Sit" just before the dog's bottom hits the floor. Ask your dog to sit before it gets anything in life it likes—going out for a walk,

below: *Teaching the "down" command is gentle and easy with a food lure.*

being petted, or groomed, or having dinner—it's the dog's way of saying "please" and "thank you."

down

- Place the food lure on your dog's nose. Lower your hand straight down to the floor, directly between the dog's front paws. Hang on to the treat by turning your palm down, with the food hidden inside your hand.
- Be patient! As your dog tries to get the

food, its head and body must lower to the floor. As soon as it flops down, give the signal that it has done the right thing, then treat. For dogs that don't catch on too quickly, pass the food or toy under a low-level chair or table, so the dog has to follow the lure underneath it by dropping down.
- Add your word command when the dog is lying down reliably for the food.

phasing out food lures

Gradually ask your pup to do more for each signal of reward and treat. This means extending how long it will sit or lie down when you ask, how far and how quickly it will run when called, and working among distractions. When all these exercises are reliable, reward the dog only for fastest responses, sometimes with food, and sometimes with praise or a toy. Keep the dog guessing about what reward will follow and it will try even harder.

left: *A 12-week-old German Shepherd is being taught to sit on command, using kind and motivational methods.*

further training

Training is an ongoing process. Starting as early as you can is no substitute for practice and expanding your dog's skills and your relationship with it.

One of the most common complaints from owners of adolescent dogs is that they pull on the leash when out for a walk. The reasons for this are numerous, but, ironically, the major one is that dogs find it very rewarding.

Imagine getting out the dog's leash before going for a walk. The chances are that the dog is already getting excited. The leash is clipped on and the dog heads toward the door, already pulling on the leash. The dog desperately wants the door to open, so it can pull the owner all the way down the walk, to the front gate. At this point it pulls to get through the gate, which is conveniently opened for the dog to push through. Having pulled all the way to the park, the dog is then let off the leash to run—the biggest reward of the dog's entire day.

Training your dog to walk happily on a loose leash takes time and patience, in sessions when you are not trying to get to the park. Start by getting your dog to follow you around the house, with the leash off to begin with. Lure it into the right position with a treat, and give your signal, then reward when it is in the right place by your side. Keep sessions short and fun.

Once you have mastered off-leash walking in the house and yard, you can attach the leash.

- Keeping the leash slack, start walking. As soon as the dog is in the right place, give your reward signal, then treat.
- Stop if you feel tension in the leash.

Only start walking again when your dog has slackened the leash—no matter how long it takes.

- After only a few repetitions of non-rewarding your dog's pulling, it should realize that pulling is counter-productive. Walking calmly, on the other hand, gets it to the park quicker.
- For some strong or very persistent pullers, a head-collar or a body harness may assist in training. Choke chains, prong collars, or other methods that teach the dog through negative or compulsive methods are not recommended, as they can cause both physical and mental damage.

"off"

"Off" means "don't touch." This is especially useful for teaching dogs not to touch food or other items unless they are told they can.

- Hold a piece of food tightly between your fingers and show it to the dog, without saying anything. If it goes to take it, say "Off" in a quiet voice and hide the food in your hand, making a fist around it.
- As soon as the dog pulls its nose away from your hand, even for a split second, give your signal of reward, say "take it" or "thank you," and give the treat.
- Practice until your dog takes its nose away instantly when you say the word.
- Start to lengthen the amount of time your dog will take its nose away from the food. Always pick the food up and give it when you are ready.

Although you can achieve a great deal of successful training at home on your own, many owners prefer to take their dog to a training class, where they can have support from the instructor and an opportunity to meet other owners. However, like people, dogs can suffer from stress, and this makes your choice of training class very important. Modern training methods, using food or toys to motivate the dogs should be used, and no force or shouting is necessary. Always go and inspect a class, without your dog, prior to joining.

below: *A dog training class gives owners an opportunity to meet others and train in a supportive atmosphere.*

the first year

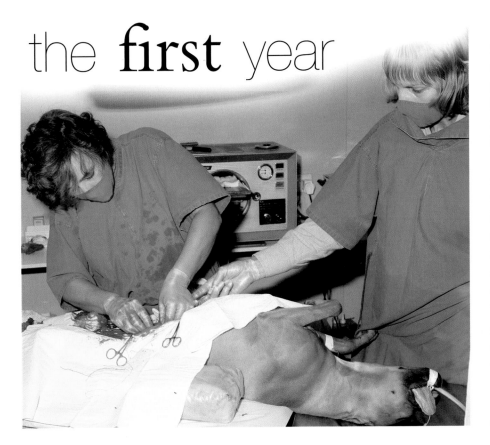

From the time that your dog loses its deciduous teeth at around 18–20 weeks, it is no longer considered a puppy. Dogs then enter a juvenile, or adolescent stage, which corresponds well to the teenage stage in human development. Just like humans, teenage dogs can be rebellious, difficult, challenging, and lovable, as they carve out their own identities and behavior traits.

Male dogs, particularly, can change quite dramatically on reaching sexual maturity. They are likely to start to lift their legs on urination, may become aggressive with other male dogs, and can show overt interest in bitches—even if they are not in season. Some may show sexual behavior toward inanimate objects, such as cushions or toys—or even other living creatures, such as visitors or the cat. It is essential that adolescent dogs continue to meet and mix with as many different dogs and people as possible, as this can be a difficult period through which socialization needs to continue.

Bitches also become sexually mature during their first year. Some may come

above: *Neutering is a sensible option for both dogs and bitches, preventing both health and behavior problems as well as unwanted litters.*

into season when they are only five months old, while others may not experience this until they are one year old. Early signs that your bitch may be coming into season are increased urination—usually small amounts in many different areas when outside, and swelling around the vulva. It is essential to keep bitches inside during their season, as their smell will be irresistible to male dogs, and they can even be followed home from a walk.

prevention of problems

Neutering prevents many different kinds of problems later in life—both behavioral and physical. Castrated males are much less likely to roam after bitches or fight with other male dogs. It also reduces the frequency with which they lift their legs, and can help in cases where a male dog is urine-marking

right: *Prevention of problems is easier than cure.*

indoors, too. Both mammary tumors and womb infections—which can be fatal—are prevented by neutering in bitches if the neutering occurs prior to the second heat, and they do not come into season again after the operation.

More dogs are given up to shelters or put to sleep during adolescence than at any other time. They no longer look like cute puppies and can be strong, uncontrollable, and even dangerous. Dogs of this age need continued training, considerable exercise, and should be kept occupied. This period passes eventually, and if the groundwork has been put in place most problems are either connected to the dog's hormonal status or are temporary.

Here are five top tips for surviving your dog's adolescence:

1. Be realistic—your dog is a dog!
2. Don't worry if it appears to have temporarily forgotten all of your previous training—the groundwork is in place.
3. Seek veterinary advice if you feel that neutering your dog would help.
4. Channel your dog's energy, rather than trying to suppress it. This means substantial exercise.
5. Keep up the good work on your dog's training and socialization—teach new tricks to keep its mind active.

behavior problems in
dogs

above: *Dog behavior counselors can shed new light on deep-seated, long-term, or serious problems.*

left: *Who is walking whom? This needs to be decided at the outset.*

Inappropriate behaviors may be irritating or even dangerous for the owner, yet perfectly natural for the dog. Understanding why the dog behaves as it does is just as important as how to modify it.

aggression to people

Aggression to human beings is the most serious behavioral problem found in dogs. Apart from pathological causes, it is nearly always a result of fear. Once threatened, dogs use one of four coping strategies to deal with the situation. These are the four Fs—Fight, Flight, Freeze, and Flirt. The option a dog picks is likely to be determined by breed characteristics, previous experience, physical health, and the context of the scenario.

For example, a dog that is terrified of men may deal with this fear by picking "Flight" as the preferred option—running away and hiding behind the furniture. However, when placed on the examination table at the vet's, and faced with a veterinarian, there is no escape. Such dogs often

"Freeze"—and stay perfectly still for a few seconds. This is an ancient strategy used by many animals in the hope that the predator won't see them—but of course it is pointless in this environment. "Flirtation"—such as bringing the person a toy, lying on your back with your legs in the air, or licking, is also unlikely to work, so finally the dog uses the only option left available—aggression or "Fight."

Once the dog realizes that such a response increases the distance between itself and the person, such behavior may increase, as it is effectively being rewarded. Add to this the owner's attempts to placate the animal, by reassuring, or to punish, which simply get associated with the presence of the threatening person, and the behavior

can easily become a habit. Aggression toward people can be triggered by many different events or circumstances—nearly always because the dog has not learned how to cope with a particular situation through socialization while young.

territorial aggression and aggression outside the home

Some dogs may be aggressive toward people coming into the home. These individuals are usually fearful of strangers, and feel more confident about defending themselves from a position within their own territory. Very rarely are these dogs protecting

below: *Avoid possessive aggression by using non-threatening preventive training.*

left: *Food-guarding behavior can be made worse by trying to remove the food bowl.*

on the bed—then show aggression when these resources are threatened when the owner attempts to move them off. Aggression can also be demonstrated over possession of items or food and this needs to be dealt with carefully if the behavior is not to increase.

Sadly, many owners teach their dogs to be aggressive over food, in the misguided belief that taking the dog's food away will teach him or her to accept it. Nothing could be further from the truth! It is easy to see why if you imagine someone coming into your dining room and taking your dinner away from you, just as you were about to start eating. You might allow this to happen once or twice, but by the third or fourth evening, you would not be very pleased to have it happen again! In order to prevent such aggression, or to treat a mild form of food guarding, adding extra-special food instead of removing the bowl usually works well. After a few repetitions, the dog starts to look hopeful when you come near the bowl—not defensive.

Aggression toward owners is also commonly caused, and exacerbated, by the use of punishment. All forms of physical punishment, such as smacking, shaking, yanking on a choke chain, the use of electric shock collars, and even shouting, are at best ineffective and at worst damaging. Punishment is never a good response if your dog's behavior is inappropriate. Instead of simply reacting, ask *why* you think the dog is acting in this way. Ask your vet for a referral to a behavior specialist as early as possible.

their owners—but they will use their owners as a second line of defense in protecting themselves and their "den."

Other dogs are fearful of unknown people or children outside the home and may use aggressive displays, such as growling or barking, to keep them away. Some mild fears about unknown people can be overcome using food or toys to form pleasant associations with them. Helpers should ensure that they use non-threatening body language when greeting an anxious dog—and avoid direct eye contact, which can be frightening to a nervous individual. However, more serious forms of aggression require early professional help from a behavior specialist. Ask your vet for a referral.

aggression toward owners

This kind of aggression is multi-faceted. Aggression may be seen in cases where dogs have enjoyed certain privileges in the home—such as getting on the furniture or sleeping

left: *This clear warning needs to be taken seriously by the owner.*

aggression to other dogs

In the wild, dogs nearly always resolve conflict or disputes between themselves without fighting. Direct physical attack creates the risk of injury—and an injured dog cannot be an effective part of the hunting team. Dogs have therefore created elaborate ways of ritualizing displays of aggression toward each other, which allow them to resolve conflict without resorting to physical attack.

The first of these signals is very subtle. Dogs generally go still, to initially indicate that they feel threatened by another dog, or are prepared to defend a resource, such as food or a resting site. If this is ignored, they may emphasize the signal by using eye contact—staring at the opponent or rolling their eyes, to show the whites.

To increase this further, they attempt to make themselves look as large as possible. Hackles may be raised (the hair on the back of the neck is erected; sometimes this extends all the way down to the tail, giving the dog an almost "hyena-like"

above: *Clear body language can diffuse aggression.*

below: *A friendly greeting between puppy and adult.*

appearance) and they may underscore the visual display with a low growl. In the event that the opponent still hasn't gotten the message, most dogs then show their teeth—drawing the lips up and back to expose a full set of weapons. A snap into the air may come next, but only as a last resort do the teeth make contact with the other dog—and even then it's unlikely that damage will be done. Only in very extreme circumstances do disputes between dogs in a natural environment escalate into full-blown fights, and even when this happens, injuries are highly unlikely, as both dogs will fight by clear and well understood rules that involve inhibited biting—where the teeth do not break the skin.

On the whole, domestic dogs are incredibly peace-loving and sociable with other dogs. Every morning dogs are taken to familiar territory—the local park, for instance—and are expected to encounter unknown dogs without showing signs of aggression. Bearing this in mind, the number of fights that occur between dogs is relatively small, and most of them are exacerbated, if not caused, by human misunderstanding, as owners try to intervene. Dogs that are well socialized with other dogs and can read their body language are excellent at keeping out of trouble, and may even play.

However, for the minority of dogs that are aggressive to other dogs, the reasons usually fall into three categories. The first of these is a lack of socialization with other dogs. Dogs learn about canine body language between the ages of four and 12 weeks. While this learning process is continued throughout life, puppies that do not have contact with lots of other

dogs before this time are already at a serious disadvantage.

A lack of socialization also leads to fear, and this is the second major cause of aggression to other dogs. A dog that is fearful may learn to be aggressive to keep other dogs at a distance—and may discover that attack is the best form of defense.

The third reason why dogs are aggressive to other dogs is because it is somehow rewarding. For some male dogs, driven by their hormonal impulses, fighting with a rival male and winning is highly rewarding. Bullying other dogs and winning those contests can start to be rewarding for some dogs in the same way as it is for playground bullies at

school. And some dogs feel rewarded by their owner's response to aggressive behavior. Ironically, while people often attempt to punish their dogs for aggression, this only makes matters worse, as the dog may associate their owner's aggression with the presence of the other dog.

To treat aggression toward other dogs, early help from an experienced behavior specialist is vital. The cause of the aggression needs to be established before treatment, and the responses of the owner need to be carefully considered. As always, prevention is better than cure, and ensuring that your puppy is well socialized with other dogs during those first critical weeks is essential.

barking

Dogs bark to attract attention, to drive other dogs or humans away, to raise the alarm, to call their "pack" together, and to indicate excitement, distress, or loneliness. Complaints about barking from neighbors top the list of dog "nuisances" and can lead to prosecution by local authorities.

barking in the home

Most dogs bark to raise the alarm when someone knocks on the front door or steps onto the driveway. This is designed to alert the "pack leaders" that there may be an intruder—but no more than that! Unfortunately, many dogs think that it is their duty to warn off every visitor to the home, as well as the mail carrier, window cleaner, and anyone else who happens to walk past the house.

Excessive barking is nearly always inflamed by the owner's reaction, since although shouting for quiet may seem logical to us, to a dog, this is simply barking encouragement! Early socialization in the home ensures that your dog is not barking through fear, but the excitement of the situation may encourage excessive noise. If this

above: *Excitement in anticipation of the owner's return can result in lots of noise.*

left: *Sociable dogs bark to gain attention from anyone willing to provide it.*

is the case in your home, rethink the situation and offer some gentle, effective training.

Teaching your dog to bark and be quiet on command is the easiest way to re-establish control when visitors arrive. This needs to be practiced in quiet moments, where there are no distractions in the early stages. Excite your dog by playing and encourage him or her to bark. Allow three "woofs," then say "shush," and immediately feed your dog some tasty treats. Very few dogs can bark and eat at the same time, so quiet behavior immediately gets reinforced. Repeat this in different rooms of the house and in the yard, until the word "shush" gets instant quiet. Gradually delay giving the food treat, so that the dog is barking and being quiet on command.

This exercise then needs to be repeated by the front door. Ring the doorbell or knock on the door. Let the dog bark three times, then say "shush" and feed. Repeat this until it is perfect. At this point you need to ask someone else to ring the doorbell. Don't immediately let them into the house, as you need to concentrate on the dog inside the front door. After a while, you can let your visitor in, keeping control of your dog by having it on the leash, if necessary. Reward it for quiet behavior, and ignore any more than three barks completely.

Another common cause of barking in the home is that the dog is suffering from a separation problem, or is barking to get attention.

barking in the car

Dogs tend to bark in the car out of sheer excitement, or because they believe that they can chase other things away from their car by doing it. The first of these reasons is frequently because the dog has come to associate trips in the car with highly pleasurable events—such as walks or visiting friends.

In order to break down this association, the dog needs to be taken out for rides in the car that are a bit more boring—around the block and straight back home, for example. Another useful trick is to confine the dog while it is in the car. Movement excites most dogs, and being able to see out of the car windows only adds to this. A traveling crate or a car harness not only helps to keep the dog calm, but makes driving safer, too!

below: *Boredom can lead to a barking habit, especially in active and demanding breeds.*

chasing

Chasing is a basic part of most dogs' normal behavior. Without being ready and able to chase, a dog in the wild would starve to death, because although dogs can eat berries and vegetation, the main bulk of their protein is gained from the meat of animals they hunt and kill. While most domestic dogs have been bred not to try to kill their "prey," many still retain a high "prey drive" and cannot resist chasing things—even if these are not other animals but joggers, cyclists, or cars.

The main culprits for chasing problems usually come from the herding group and the sighthounds. Collies and Shepherds are the most likely to chase, simply because they have been bred for many centuries for their ability to follow a very specialized sequence of behavior: "eye, stalk, and chase." This means that the dog "locks on" to an object or animal, stalks it with body low to the ground to avoid being seen, then rushes at the "prey" in an attempt to catch it. Collies, in particular, tend to want to chase people—then do one of two things if they manage to catch them: either circle them to keep them still, or keep "worrying" them to move them on.

above: *Chasing is an extremely rewarding activity for many breeds.*

below: *Redirect instinctive behaviors to both dog and owner's advantage.*

behavior to a more acceptable outlet. For those who don't have a flock of sheep at their disposal to give the dog a natural outlet, teaching the dog to chase toys and increasing training for control can be effective.

This needs to be done in a very structured way. The dog needs to learn that it can chase toys when you allow it, but must also stop chasing on command. An instant "down," and a reliable recall are also vital. These exercises are best practiced with an experienced and accredited dog trainer, who will be able to structure a training program for you.

Dogs that attempt to round up people, children, or other animals in the house can also be taught to "herd" in a more appropriate way—and often require more mental stimulation generally. Many active, working dogs become "self-employed" if they are not given enough to do!

For some dogs, such as ex-racing Greyhounds and some herding dogs, the temptation to chase livestock, other dogs, small animals, or people is just too great to modify. In these instances, it is sensible to maintain control of the dog, by keeping it on the leash. Although this may seem frustrating, many dogs can lead perfectly happy and contented lives on-leash, if a little thought and imagination goes into their daily outings. Walking is as much about mental stimulation as it is physical exercise. Tracking, finding "lost" articles, and retrieving games can all be played on the leash, as can playing with toys and basic "agility"— jumping over and walking along natural obstacles.

If your dog cannot be let off the leash for whatever reason, you need to put extra effort into your relationship with your dog and provide extra interaction when you are out for walks. You will both reap the benefits.

Sighthounds, such as Greyhounds and Afghan Hounds, are nearly always aroused by the sight of a fast-moving animal or person, and can be persistent cat and squirrel chasers. Terriers are also prone to chasing. As vermin hunters their drive to chase after and catch small prey is strong—and ankles or children are sometimes chased as a substitute.

Chasing is such a basic, instinctive behavior that it is usually impossible to cure the dog of the habit. Management of the problem is nearly always centered around redirection of the

fear behaviors— phobias and nervousness

Some of the most problematic canine behaviors arise from fear. Aggression is nearly always an active means of coping with fear, but other reactions also arise. Some fearful dogs attempt to cope with a "crisis" by behaving in a passive way. These dogs typically show submissive body language, with ears down and tail tucked under. They may crouch to become as small as possible and may also shake and salivate with fear. Such dogs often try to flee from a situation they find threatening, or may simply freeze.

Although many owners think that their dog must have had a bad experience in order to be fearful of someone or something, it is far more common for fear to arise from a lack of experience. Social or environmental deprivation between four and 12 weeks is the classic cause. Dogs that are born and raised in a barn, for example, may not have been exposed to the sounds, smells, or sights of a normal domestic home—and therefore show fearful reactions when seeing the vacuum cleaner for the first time, or hearing a vehicle. Over time, some dogs learn to cope with these stimuli, but equally common are those whose fears simply get worse and worse without treatment. Indeed, the "generalization" of fears and phobias is a great risk—for the dog that is initially fearful of loud noises outside may develop a fear of them inside as well.

Phobias are extreme fears. Usually, phobias start as a result of a fear about a particular stimulus. For example, a dog that has not heard loud noises in puppyhood is bound to be startled by explosions, such as fireworks, the first time it hears them. Each and every time this noise is heard thereafter, the dog will attempt to escape or hide, and it may salivate, pant, and shake. For all intents and purposes, this dog is experiencing what humans would describe as a panic attack.

Some new advances in veterinary medicine have been developed to deal with phobias, particularly firework and thunder phobias. Such drug support always needs to be prescribed by a veterinarian and given in conjunction with a behavioral program. However, owners can often do much to ease

their dogs' fears and ensure that phobias do not become any worse over time.

Ironically, nearly all severe phobias are created by the owner's reaction to the dog's initial fear. Dogs are not small children, and although we would try to reassure a child with soothing words and gentle caresses if they were frightened, this is probably the worst possible thing that an owner can do for a dog if it is anxious. This is because dogs do not understand the words that we are saying, but instead hear something akin to "Good dog for being scared," and respond to their owner's anxiety about the situation, too. This confirms in the dog's mind that it was right to be fearful in the first place, and reinforces its behavior. Very few other animals are terrified of thunder, fireworks, or other loud noises. Although they may be startled by them, and move away, their fear is not reinforced or rewarded, so they remain calm.

If your dog has never shown fear at loud noises or unusual experiences, make sure you keep it that way, by associating pleasant things with such events and ignoring any kind of reaction to them. For example, the first time that a puppy hears a loud noise, such as thunder, it is natural for it to run and hide. If you can steel yourself to ignore this completely, and carry on with whatever you were doing, your puppy will follow your example and believe that it was nothing to be frightened of. Then you can systematically reward brave behavior by playing games, feeding, or giving treats.

If your dog already shows fear behavior during fireworks or thunderstorms, try to ignore it as much as you can. Provide an area where your dog can hide, to satisfy his "denning" instincts, and remain calm yourself. Do not attempt to coax your dog out with food or try to reassure it—it will simply interpret this as a reward for the behavior. Instead, wait until the dog shows more confidence, then reward this with praise and food.

separation problems

Some of the most common behavior problems in dogs of all ages are the result of being left alone at home. Dogs with separation problems may howl or bark to attempt to call the rest of their "pack" home again, become destructive—tearing or clawing at carpets, objects, furniture, or walls and doors—or they may lose bowel or bladder control. In extreme cases, some dogs have been known to become so distressed at being left alone that they self-mutilate—biting at themselves until the affected area becomes sore and infected.

Separation problems tend to fall into three broad categories:

1. separation anxiety or separation distress

Dogs that suffer from separation anxiety simply cannot cope when they are left alone at home, and chew or howl in order to make themselves feel better—a little like people who

bite their fingernails when under stress. Such dogs are nearly always overattached to their owners when they are at home—following them from room to room like shadows, and this is the basis of the problem. Such

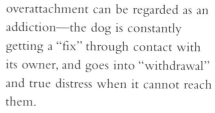

above: *Bored dogs will find their own amusement—usually to the consternation of their owners.*

overattachment can be regarded as an addiction—the dog is constantly getting a "fix" through contact with its owner, and goes into "withdrawal" and true distress when it cannot reach them.

Over time, this dog needs to learn that there are times when it cannot have contact with the owner, even when they are in the house together. Clear signals of reward (you may have contact) and non-reward (no contact allowed for a short period) need to be instigated, and the period of time that the dog is without the owner gradually extended from only a few seconds, to minutes, then an hour. The solution to this problem always needs to be gradual and carefully structured, preferably with the help of a behavior specialist.

left: *Self-mutilation can be a result of stress.*

2. separation frustration

Some dogs do not believe their owners have the right to go out and leave them! These dogs then become frustrated, and relieve this frustration through becoming destructive, noisy, or messing in the house.

They tend to be demanding in other ways too—often taking control of time, attention, or resources when the owner is home. Reestablishing the rules and boundaries of the relationship can help greatly, but this is best done with the advice of a behavior counselor.

3. boredom and lack of mental stimulation

In the wild, dogs would be required to solve problems all day long. Finding and hunting for food, maintaining social interactions, running and walking great distances, keeping territory safe, finding places to rest, and watching out for predators or intruders would all be part of an average day's work.

In a domestic situation, the dog's food is provided and placed in a dish for him to eat. Its exercise and play times are limited by the owner, who decides the length of time and type of interaction, and few intruders are anticipated. It's little wonder that so many dogs show signs of boredom, particularly when left alone at home. Given sufficient time and opportunity, bored dogs problem-solve to their heart's content—but usually to the consternation of their owners on return. Many dogs learn how to open doors, turn knobs, open the fridge door to raid the contents, find forbidden items to chew or eat, and generally use the house as an amusement arcade!

If you suspect that your dog is bored when left alone, you need to provide more stimulation for it both when you are at home and for when you go out. Increased exercise is usually recommended, as a tired dog is less likely to get into trouble. However, leaving your dog with some exciting toys to play with and some novelty items to explore may also help. "Interactive" toys, which dispense food while the dog is playing with them, are ideal, as are chews. Even a large cardboard box can be a fun object to play with—especially since it won't matter if your dog destroys it.

below: *Mental exercise is every bit as important as physical exercise for a domestic dog, but an "addiction" to contact should be avoided.*

sexual problems

Nothing is more embarrassing than taking your dog to someone else's home and watching it lift its leg against the furniture! Nothing, that is, except having to pull your dog off some unsuspecting visitor whose leg is being passionately embraced by your eager Labrador!

Nearly all sexual problems in domestic dogs are found in males. Although some bitches will mark using urine just before coming into season, and a few mount people or other dogs as a social signal of dominance or as an effective means of attention-seeking, on the whole, adolescent males are the prime culprits.

All male dogs experience a surge of testosterone, the male hormone, around adolescence. This equates to puberty in human beings and has some similar effects! Males may become prone to running away to hunt for bitches. They may become aggressive toward other male dogs and may try to

above: *Any time, any place, anywhere—dogs are great opportunists!*

left: *An overt signal. This Border Collie has sex on his mind!*

test their strength with other dogs, or even with members of their human "pack."

Uncastrated males typically learn to lift their legs at this stage—to squirt a urine "message" as high as possible on vertical surfaces for other dogs to "read." This is a social signal to other dogs that a male is in the territory and probably gives information about social status, hormonal status, and physical health. They also become much more interested in the urine marks left by other dogs—both male and female. This can make taking the dog for a walk somewhat tiring, as you get dragged from tree to tree and streetlight to streetlight.

Sexual development causes many young dogs to try to experiment with sex. Some will try to mount other dogs while out in the park, although most discover that their advances are not welcome. Others take the safer option, and mount inanimate objects such as cushions, soft toys, or even the curtains. A few dogs even try to mount other creatures in the same household. Long-suffering cats may take the brunt of these advances, while in other cases, children or even adults can become the object of the dog's desire.

While such overt sexual behavior nearly always diminishes in most adolescent dogs as they pass into true adulthood, for some the urge to procreate never fades, and they live a frustrated and frustrating existence. For owners who wish to avoid the "teenage" stage altogether, early neutering of their dog is highly recommended. Castration before the age of 9–12 months usually prevents such problems as hypersexuality, wander-lust, mounting, excessive leg-lifting outside, and indoor urination—either in your home or someone else's. Neutering is rarely a cure for a behavioral problem, but research has shown that in dogs that are exclusively aggressive to other male dogs, it can often help a great deal. Castration is a simple procedure and is likely to keep your male dog out of trouble, while reducing frustration for him as well.

below: *Pawing can be a precursor to mounting—and even human legs can sometimes seem all too attractive!*

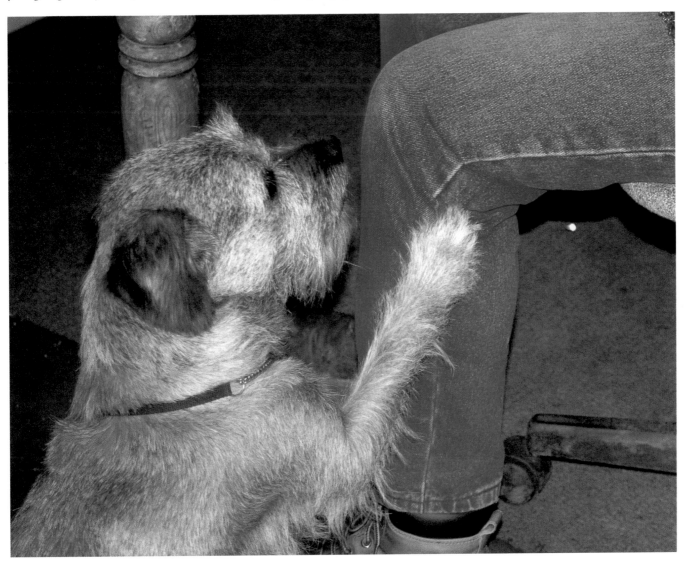

stealing **food** and **other** items

Dogs are one of the most adaptable and evolutionarily successful creatures on earth. One of the reasons for this is that they are expert scavengers. Any food, unless it is actually in the mouth of another pack member, is up for grabs—if it's available, it's worth having!

On the whole, domestic dogs have not lost this drive to scavenge. If they find food or something that they regard as edible, and they get the chance, they are likely to eat it. This is not naughty behavior or stealing from the dog's point of view—but a sensible use of resources. Unfortunately, humans have different values and we are not sympathetic if we discover that the dog has jumped up on the kitchen counter and eaten the Sunday roast, or put its head in the garbage can and licked it clean.

The desire to scavenge is usually governed to some extent by breed characteristics. Gundogs are notorious

"stomachs-on-legs" and will usually eat anything and everything if given the chance. Scavenging also depends on the diet that the dog is currently eating, and the allure of the food it finds. Nearly all dogs find the dung of other animals almost impossible to resist. Cat feces, horse manure, cattle dung, rabbit and fox droppings are all considered to be doggie delicacies, even if we don't agree! Although repulsive to us, such morsels are unlikely to do your

above: *By ignoring "begging" an owner can easily teach their dog that human food is not for sharing.*

left: *Dogs' gastronomic delights are often very different from our own!*

above: *Dogs are natural scavengers, so prevention rather than cure works best.*

dog any harm as long as you regularly have your dog wormed.

Prevention is always better than cure if you have a dog that would like to spend ten hours a day eating. Keeping the dog out of the kitchen while cooking, teaching it to lie in a bed or basket with a chew or toy during family mealtimes, and putting food out of reach are all sensible strategies. If the dog manages to obtain food only occasionally, the lure of trying to get it is even stronger. This makes a "no feeding from the table" rule even more important.

In most domestic households, dogs have access to many different kinds of objects, some of which they are allowed to touch and others they are

forbidden to pick up. Childrens' toys, remote control units, eyeglasses, hair bands, socks, even Christmas decorations are all removed from dogs' stomachs by veterinarians every year, and many dogs are killed after ingesting poisons, such as human medication and household chemicals.

It is perfectly normal for a puppy to want to pick up objects and put them in its mouth. Much like human toddlers, puppies explore the world around them through taste and smell, as well as testing to see what the reaction from those around them will be. This is usually the prime reason dogs "steal" items from around the house.

Imagine the scenario: your dog is lying quietly on the floor, chewing on a dog toy that you have given it. What do you do or say? Very little! Now

imagine the same dog lying on the floor quietly chewing your wallet. The reaction would be somewhat different. Dogs, like children, will work hard to get attention, even negative attention, such as being scolded. Most young or adolescent dogs love nothing better than watching their owners getting hot under the collar, and if they can turn possession of a forbidden item into a chase game around the house and into the yard—even better! In this way, dogs soon learn that chewing their own toy gets no rewards, attention, or excitement at all, while picking up and chewing a valuable object results in the equivalent of winning the lottery.

The best solution for this kind of behavior is to reverse the reaction you give to the dog. If it picks up one of its own toys, show excitement, play, and praise. On the other hand, if it picks up an object you don't want it to have, but can sacrifice, such as a tissue or a newspaper, walk straight out of the room without a word. If the object is one that you really can't ignore, creating a distraction, such as ringing the front doorbell, gives you a window of opportunity to retrieve it, without inadvertently giving the dog attention for unwanted behavior. Any aggression over possession of stolen articles should be dealt with in conjunction with a behavior specialist.

above: *If you don't want it chewed, don't leave it lying around! Give the puppy an acceptable alternative to chew.*

training problems

There are a number of training problems that can occur with any type or age of dog. Some of these simply require an understanding of why the dog is performing the behavior and ensuring that alternative, more appropriate behavior is reinforced instead, while others may require the help of an experienced trainer to resolve.

not coming back when called

This is probably the number one dog training problem. Dogs may run off to meet other dogs, sniff the grass, chase squirrels, or simply avoid going home. All dogs that are allowed to run freely off the leash should be taught an effective recall, not only to prevent them from becoming a nuisance to others, but also for their own safety.

From the dog's point of view, coming back to its owner when off the leash is a negative experience. Commonly, owners get angry when the dog fails to return, and verbally or physically punish the dog when it eventually does. This only makes it even more determined to keep away from the owner next time! For other dogs who have more enlightened owners, coming back when called simply means the end of the walk—the leash is put on and the fun is at an end. This can be a psychological punishment—and discourages the dog from coming back in the future.

In order to establish good recalls, your dog needs to know that you are the most exciting thing in the park—better than all the squirrels, other dogs, and wonderful smells put together. Teaching your dog to come when called at home, in the house, then in the yard will help initially. Give the dog praise, food, and games with toys

to start to build its belief that you really are exciting to be with. Gradually practice this in more and more distracting environments—and eventually in the park.

jumping up

Dogs usually jump up in order to get closer to a human face when they are greeting them. This is a friendly gesture, and to respond to it with aggression or anger will not only be inappropriate, but highly confusing for the dog. Most dogs persist in jumping up at people because they get rewarded for doing it. Even negative attention is better than no attention at all, and causing a

right: *Dogs jump up for many reasons, but the prime one is inappropriate greeting behavior.*

they can be held on a leash in the initial stages.

• As soon as the dog puts all four feet, or even better, its bottom, on the floor, the person rewards the dog—with food, toys, or praise and attention.

• If the front feet come off the floor again, immediately fold arms and turn away, to non-reward the behavior.

• Repeat this in as many different places and with as many different people as possible.

• Your dog will soon discover that sitting gets attention, and even food treats, while jumping up is a waste of energy and gets nothing.

below: *Even small dogs benefit from some "creative" training—you will be surprised at just what they can do.*

person to squeal as their stockings get damaged, or to engage in a struggle to push the dog away as their suit gets dirtied by muddy paws, is truly exciting for the dog.

A dog cannot jump up if it is sitting. Teaching a dog to "sit to greet" is the easiest way to prevent this unwanted behavior, without confrontation or raised blood pressure. To teach this new behavior, the dog must understand that jumping up gets no rewards, while sitting wins the jackpot.

Follow these simple rules to reeducate your dog when greeting people:

• All jumping up is ignored completely. The person needs to fold their arms and turn away, effectively "blanking" the unwanted behavior. If the dog is particularly large or strong,

miscellaneous problems

digging

Many dogs love to dig, particularly terriers, which have been bred for centuries to do exactly that. Although digging is unacceptable to us, it is perfectly normal canine behavior, and as such is often better redirected than cured. Creating a digging area for confirmed canine gardeners is usually the best way of offering an appropriate outlet for the behavior, without having a hole the size of a swimming pool in your lawn.

Choose an appropriate site, then dig a large area, adding builder's sand to the soil, so that it won't clog in the dog's paws too much. Take your dog to the pit and let it watch you bury a juicy bone, a toy that it really likes, or some biscuits, then let it dig them up. Repeat this a few times, then bury such items in the digging area once or twice a week when the dog is not around. Having found treasure in this spot, very few dogs will want to dig elsewhere.

chewing

Puppies need to chew in order to relieve the pressure on their gums as their new teeth come in at around 18–24 weeks of age. Providing objects to chew is therefore vital if you don't want the pup to chew your best furniture. Placing toys and chews in the fridge or even the freezer before offering them can really help to soothe sore gums, too.

Later on, the adult teeth also set into the bone of the jaw, and this can cause more teething trouble at around eight months. Other chewing can be due to boredom, an inappropriate diet, or stress.

below: *Rolling may be used to disguise a dog's own scent, or just because it feels good!*

rolling

One minute your dog is frolicking happily in the grass in the local park, the next it has thrown itself on the ground and is in rapture rolling in something so foul that you can hardly bear to walk it home! Dogs often love to roll in strong-smelling objects—the feces of other animals and the carcasses of dead birds and mammals.

The reason for this behavior is still unknown, but several theories exist. Some maintain that the dog draws more attention to itself from other dogs—a kind of perfume or aftershave effect. Others believe that this behavior harks back to the hunting instincts of wild dogs—in order to stalk prey without detection, dogs would roll in the feces of the prey animal, masking their own smell on

the wind. We will probably never know the reason why dogs do this, but one thing is certain—they nearly always seem to time it to happen just after a bath!

Shadow chasing and tail chasing

Seen most in Collies and other herding breeds, shadow chasing may appear to be amusing at first, but can result in severe behavioral problems. The first manifestation of this unusual behavior is usually seen as the dog jumps on a shadow on the floor, tries to dig at it with the front paws, or tries to bite it as it moves. Sadly, this problem is often triggered by children playing with a flashlight beam, and laughing as the dog tries to "catch" it. In some dogs this behavior can become so addictive that it develops into an obsession, meaning that the

above: *Tail chasing may seem amusing to some owners, but can develop into a serious behavioral disorder.*

dog cannot rest or behave normally, but spends all its time hunting for shadows.

Tail chasing can occur in the same way—dogs love laughter, and watching a puppy spin around and try to catch its own tail may be funny to begin with, but can soon become an obsession, or an addictive attention-seeking behavior. Ignoring such stereotypical behavior patterns at the outset is usually the best way of preventing their development. However, in some individuals, such behaviors can indicate a deeper disturbance, or even a physiological problem. Ask your vet for advice.

above: *First aid is vital after an accident. Emergency veterinary treatmeny may then be required.*

right: *An eye exam requires concentration.*

Animals, like humans, suffer from a variety of ailments—from overeating to old age, from diarrhea to broken limbs. Yet many illnesses and accidents can be prevented by understanding and anticipating the health and medical needs of your dog.

canine
health

choosing a vet

In an ideal world, all pet owners would be registered with a veterinarian of their choice. A common misconception is that vets deal only with sick animals, and many people's first contact with a veterinarian is in an emergency. It is common for a vet to be woken up in the wee hours by an owner who is not registered as a client because their pet "has never been ill before." However grateful you may be for the help given, this is not the best time either to form a meaningful relationship with the sleep-deprived veterinarian or to assess objectively the facilities and services available to you.

For routine care, the main criterion for choice of veterinarian is usually that of convenience. How close is the clinic to where you live? What are the consulting hours and will you be seen

below: *Minor ear ailments are common. The vet will need to make a close examination.*

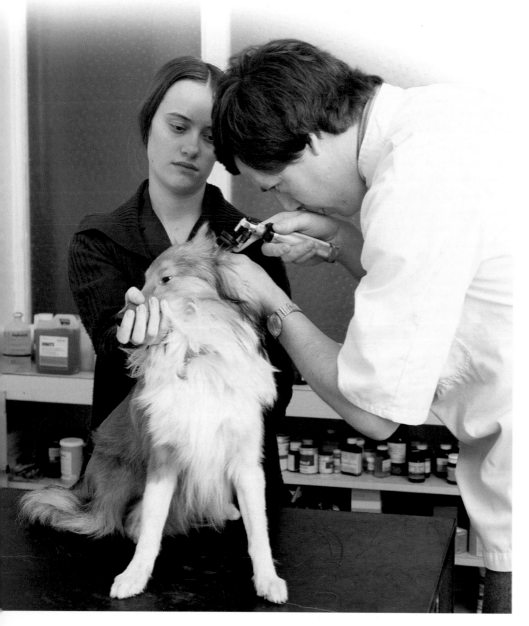

by appointment? Most important, how much does it all cost?

Once you have registered, other factors will be taken into consideration. How friendly were the receptionists? Were you seen on time? Was the vet approachable and did you feel satisfied with the advice and treatment given? Were you given value for your money?

Many practices offer a wide range of services to aid diagnosis (laboratory facilities such as blood tests, X-ray, and ultrasound equipment, for example) and to complement the health of your pet (grooming facilities and over-the-counter sales of health care products). Clinics may be held to give advice about weight problems, the special needs of the older animal, and dealing with problem behaviors. A specially built, brand new building may indicate a willingness on the part of the vets to invest income in up-to-date, "state of the art" premises and equipment. It may also mean, however, that as a multi-vet practice it can be difficult to see the same vet twice and the service may seem impersonal.

You may prefer a smaller, less "high-tech" building with a more personal atmosphere, and it does not necessarily matter how limited a vet's in-house facilities are, as long as external help is readily sought if needed. Many specialist veterinary referral services are now available in all disciplines, both at veterinary schools and in private practice, and a conscientious veterinarian should be willing to use these services if the demands of a case exceed what he can offer.

Do not feel embarrassed if you want to ask for a second opinion from another veterinarian or specialist, or if you feel complementary therapies such as homeopathy would benefit your animal. Such referrals should be arranged with the prior knowledge of your vet, who should provide a letter of referral with any relevant history. He in turn should be given full details of any specialist advice or treatment given so that your pet can benefit from complete continuity of care.

In some countries veterinary practices are obliged to provide a 24-hour emergency service for their clients, and you should check to find out if this is the case in your country. Always telephone your own veterinarian first if you need emergency advice. A practice with which you are not registered should only see you if your normal vet is unavailable for some reason. Try to limit your calls to normal business hours whenever possible. The vet you speak to at 4 AM will usually have had a full day at work and will have another normal day ahead of him. Many so-called emergencies are cases that have deteriorated for lack of earlier treatment. A request to be seen outside of normal office hours will be viewed more favorably if not preceded with a description of symptoms that first appeared two weeks ago!

The income generated by routine health care and preventive treatment,

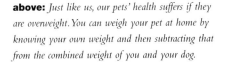

both medical and surgical, subsidizes the cost of more specialist facilities, including after-hours care. When considering the cost of yearly vaccinations, for example, it should be realized that a proportion of this fee may enable the practice to be available

above: *Just like us, our pets' health suffers if they are overweight. You can weigh your pet at home by knowing your own weight and then subtracting that from the combined weight of you and your dog.*

24 hours a day for 365 days a year. It may therefore be a false economy to "shop around" for the cheapest vaccination or neutering operation. In addition, a veterinary hospital is covered by more stringent regulations and requirements than a normal veterinary practice and the costs involved in the upkeep of such premises may justify higher charges. The aim of all veterinary practices should be the establishment of a long-term relationship with their clients to mutual benefit, which will enable knowledgable supervision of all pets' health care needs.

left: *Giving medication takes practice and care.*

when to go to your vet

There is enormous variation in the criteria pet owners use when deciding whether a trip to the vet is necessary. A cough may have been evident for six weeks or just six hours. The dog may have vomited twice yesterday or many times over several weeks. The lump causing concern may need a magnifying glass to be seen, or be so large as to make surgical removal very difficult, if not impossible.

Delay in seeking advice is sometimes caused by concerns regarding how much the necessary treatment will cost.

below: *Waiting for the vet. Good, calm behavior in the office is important for dogs.*

Ironically, this can have the effect of making the case more complex than it needed to have been and therefore more expensive. On other occasions, particularly in the older animal, the assumption is made that the condition is incurable or that nothing can be done to alleviate the symptoms and that the only advice will be to put the animal to sleep. Unfortunately, this delay can indeed result in euthanasia being the only option, although the condition might have responded to treatment if only the dog had been seen sooner.

As a general rule, if a symptom is causing concern, the sooner you consult a vet, the better. The

consultation will either allay unnecessary fears about a condition or enable prompt action to be taken to start investigation or treatment. All vets should provide an estimate of the cost of any proposed treatment so that any financial worries can be discussed. You may be able to pay by installments, as long as prior arrangement is made, and certain charities may provide help in needy cases.

You should contact your veterinarian regarding any worrying symptoms that do not abate within two to three days. Symptoms that may cause concern include increased sleepiness or lethargy, unwillingness to exercise, reduced

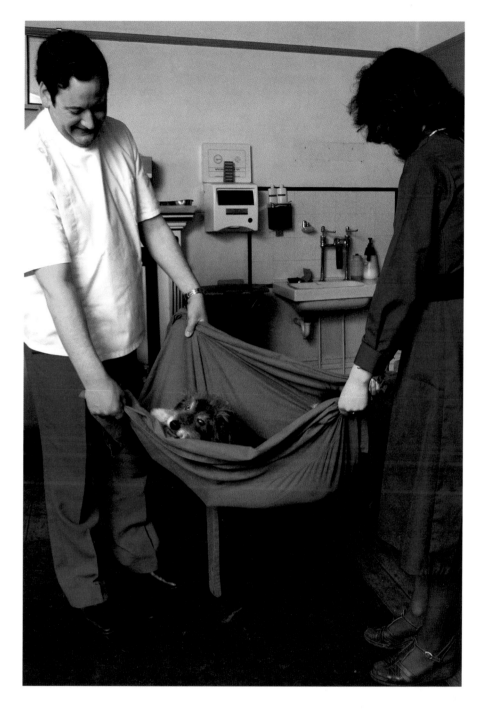

animal before advice can be given.

Even if the hospital is fully booked, every effort should be made by your vet to examine a sick or injured animal, even if it means routine appointments may be delayed. In return, it will be appreciated if you make the necessary arrangements to come to the hospital at the time specified, even if this means some inconvenience, such as taking time off work or arranging child care.

Certain conditions, such as diabetes or epilepsy, need permanent medication for which repeat prescriptions are necessary. Such animals must be examined by a vet at least once a year. Some conditions require more frequent examinations.

appetite, or an increase in thirst, vomiting, or diarrhea, coughing, or breathlessness, and any change in the normal behavior or demeanor of the animal. Any skin wounds noticed should be seen within 24 hours. Even if they do not need suturing, prompt administration of antibiotics is necessary in many cases to prevent infection. This is particularly important if your dog has been bitten, as infection is almost inevitable. Any dog that has been involved in a traffic accident should be seen as soon as possible, even if the injuries seem relatively minor. Certain traumatic conditions are not immediately apparent and it may be advisable to keep such cases in for observation.

For minor ailments, such as diarrhea, advice may be given on the telephone without the need for a consultation. However, if there is any doubt as to the severity of the problem and particularly in very young or old animals, a vet's obligation is always to examine the

preventive health care

Vaccination programs are of crucial importance in keeping four major diseases of dogs at bay—distemper, hepatitis, leptospirosis, and the most recent to emerge, canine parvovirus. Most vaccines also include parainfluenza virus, which is one of the causes of the syndrome previously known as kennel cough and now more accurately termed infectious bronchitis. Thanks to vaccination, these diseases are now rare. For complete protection, a dog should be vaccinated twice in puppyhood and booster injections given thereafter as recommended by your veterinarian.

The annual booster also provides the opportunity for your dog to have a thorough clinical examination, including eyes, skin, and teeth—in fact the equivalent of a major car service! Typical conditions picked up during routine examination include arthritis, lumps and bumps of various descriptions, and very important, dental disease. If these are diagnosed and dealt with early, much chronic discomfort can be prevented. Your vet may recommend a routine urine or blood test, often invaluable in the older dog, to detect problems such as early liver or kidney dysfunction.

It is generally accepted that if a dog is not to be used for breeding, neutering is a sensible option, not only to reduce the number of unwanted puppies, but also to prevent potentially life-threatening illnesses,

below: *For external ear infections, veterinarians will usually use a liberal amount of antibiotic, anti-inflammatory, and anti-parasitic ear drops to check further damage.*

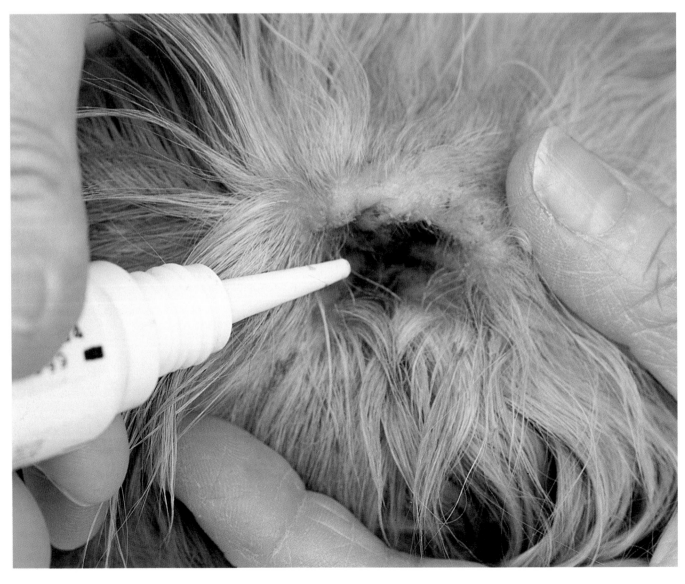

left: *Maintain hygienic standards when dealing with your dog's health. Any external ailment it may be suffering from could easily be passed on to you if you do not take proper precautions.*

such as testicular cancer and womb infections. There is now considerable evidence to suggest that spaying a bitch at around six months of age before she has her first season can substantially reduce the chances of mammary cancer when she is older. In addition, neutered animals may be considerably more content when free of their sex drive in the relatively unnatural conditions in which we expect them to live!

fleas

Fleas have been around for 40 million years and have had plenty of time to adapt and develop into a highly successful parasite! In addition to causing problems of their own, such as skin irritation, allergic reactions, and even anemia if present in large numbers, they act as the intermediate host for the dog and cat tapeworm, *Dipylidium caninum*.

Contrary to popular opinion, flea transmission between animals outdoors is uncommon, as temperatures are generally too low for their survival. The vast majority of fleas live and breed in the warm, protected environment we provide for ourselves—our centrally heated and deep-pile carpeted homes.

Because the number of fleas seen on your dog is generally just the tip of a parasitic iceberg, it is essential that insecticidal preparations are used in the dog's environment, as well as on the dog itself. These usually take the form of long-acting sprays, whereas the most effective and convenient insecticides for the dog are monthly applications of one of a number of "topical" preparations that are absorbed into the top layer of skin.

In addition, a non-insecticidal method of flea control is now available that effectively acts as a contraceptive for fleas and is given to your dog once a month in tablet form. The drug prevents development of the egg into the larval flea and can

be safely given either on its own or, more effectively, in combination with an insecticide.

The most effective insecticides are available only by prescription from your veterinarian, so be aware that you may be asked to bring your dog in for a health check before the drug can be supplied. In addition, cats and dogs share the same species of flea, most commonly *Ctenocephalides felis*, so that the same preparations must be used on all dogs and cats that they regularly encounter.

The life cycle of the flea

Fleas can be successfully controlled before they reach the cycle of adulthood and begin to feed off your dog. However, ensure that if you choose to have your pet wear a flea collar that the dog is not allergic to it.

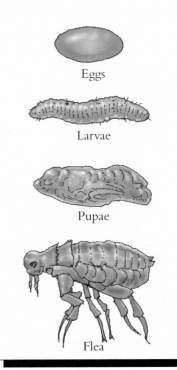

Eggs

Larvae

Pupae

Flea

worms

An effective multi-wormer should be routinely administered three or four times per year to all dogs, and more frequently when there is higher risk of infection, such as when in close contact with litters of puppies. Regular worming not only prevents worm-related damage to the dog itself, but also prevents accidental infection of humans, particularly children.

Diseases that are communicable between animals and humans are called *zoonoses* (see page 134) and, if one were to believe some anti-dog lobbyists, it is surprising that man survives contact with dogs at all! In reality, the number of diseases that can be contracted by humans from animals is relatively few, for the simple reason that the various species have very different normal body temperatures. This renders our bodies inhospitable to most organisms adapted to dog tissues, which are warmer.

The table below summarizes the main species of worms found in dogs. The two worm species of zoonotic importance, *Toxocara canis* and *Echinococcus granulosus*, are marked with an asterisk.

The life cycle of the roundworm, *Toxacara canis*, involves the migration of immature larval forms through the body of the dog before they mature to adults in the dog's intestines. Infection is picked up by the ingestion of worm eggs passed out in the feces of an infected dog, and this is one of the ways a puppy becomes infected by its mother.

If a child accidentally eats worm eggs, the larvae migrate through the body as they would in the dog but, instead of maturing to adult form in the gut, they settle in body tissues such as lung, liver, or kidney and cause the condition known as *human toxocariasis*. If the larvae happen to settle in the eye—a condition known as *ocular larva migrans*—impaired vision can result. It should be stressed that, although this condition has received much media attention, it is relatively rare—only one case per million people is diagnosed each year. The eggs do not become infective until two weeks after passage, so keeping your puppy well-groomed and clearing feces up immediately will greatly reduce the risk of infection. Once deposited in the environment, however, the eggs can remain infective for several years.

Eggs of the tapeworm, *Echinococcus granulosus*, passed out in dog feces, form hydatid cysts in the internal organs of the sheep and horse. Dogs become infected in turn if fed, or by scavenging, the raw offal, particularly liver and lungs, from such animals.

Hydatid disease in man results when a human replaces the sheep or horse in the life cycle by accidentally eating *Echinococcus* eggs from an infected dog. The resulting cysts on organs such as the liver, lungs, spleen, and kidney have in the past frequently needed surgical removal, but drug therapy can now be effective in sterilizing the cysts. The disease is most common in sheep-farming areas, but may also occur around slaughterhouses where dogs have access to infected offal.

NEMATODES

Roundworms
Species: *Toxocara canis*★/*Toxocara leonina*
Found in all dogs.
Source of infection: eggs passed out in feces of infected dog.

Hookworms
Species: *Uncinariastenocephala Ancylostomacaninum*
Found in kennel or pack dogs.
Source of infection: eggs passed out in feces of infected dog.

Whipworms
Species: *Trichuris vulpis*
Found in kennel or pack dogs.
Source of infection: eggs passed out in feces of infected dog.

Lungworms
Species: *Filiaroides osleri Angiostrongylus abstrusus*
Found in kennel and pack dogs.
Source of infection: eggs passed out in feces of infected dog.

CESTODES

Tapeworms
Species: *Dipylidium caninum*
Found in all dogs.
Source of infection: larvae carried in fleas.

Species: *Taenia ovis, Taenia hydatigena, Taenia pisiformis, Taenia multiceps*
Found mainly in sheepdogs that are fed uncooked offal.
Source of infection: sheep, pig, cow, or rabbit meat.

Species: *Echinococcus granulosus*★/*Echinococcus multilocularis*
Found in sheep dogs or those fed uncooked offal.
Source of infection: cysts in offal of sheep and horse.

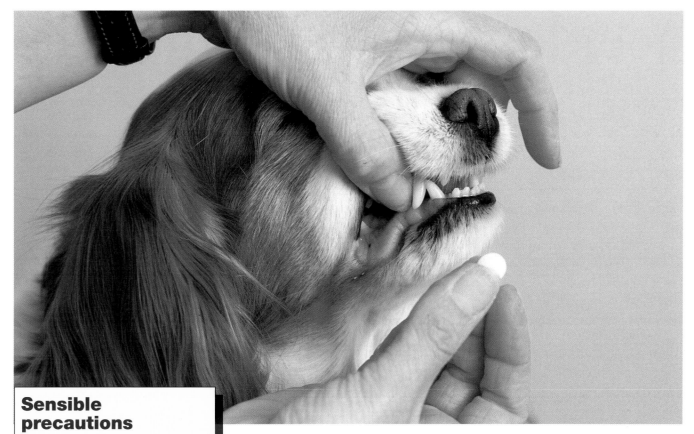

Sensible precautions

1. Worm all newly acquired puppies. Worm all adults between two and four times a year.
2. Practice rigorous hygiene. Always wash hands after handling dogs and before eating.
3. Be scrupulous about disposal of dog feces using poop scoops, etc.
4. Do not allow your dog into children's play areas in public parks.

Bacteria such as *Salmonella* and *Campylobacter* may cause gastrointestinal disease in both dogs and humans, but the infection may be from a common source (the same contaminated take-out meal) rather than transmission from dog to human.

Ringworm is a fungal infection of the skin, not common in dogs, but it can be readily picked up by humans. The infection in man forms a red ring on the skin, from which the organism gets its name.

heartworm

Infection with heartworm (*Dirofilaria immitis*) is seen in dogs in many parts of the world. Transmission of heartworm is through mosquito bites. Heartworm infection can cause heart, lung, and brain disease. In areas where heartworm infection is relatively common, dogs can be given medication to prevent infection.

above: *Regularly administering worming pills to your dog—in accordance with instructions from your vet—can maintain its health.*

below: *Medication must always be given according to veterinary instruction and kept out of reach of pets and children.*

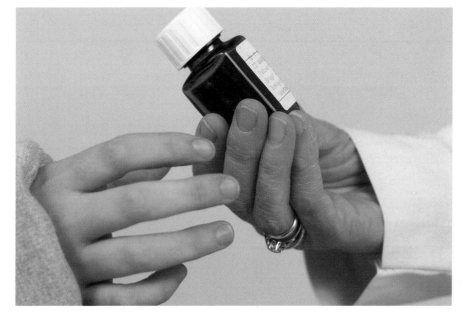

accidents and emergencies

If you think you have a case that constitutes an emergency, always telephone your veterinarian's office first for advice. This is particularly important after normal business hours, when the veterinarian on duty is unlikely to be on the premises. If a nurse is present, as in a veterinary hospital, he or she will usually have been given instructions, for security reasons, not to open the door unless the vet on duty has informed them that an emergency is on its way. Much delay and misunderstanding can therefore be avoided by an initial telephone call.

If the vet advises immediate attention, you will nearly always be asked to take the dog directly to the office or clinic, where staff and equipment necessary for the treatment of emergency cases are readily available.

traffic accidents

Any dog involved in a traffic accident, even with apparently minor injuries, should be checked over, as soon as possible, as internal bleeding may

below: *Shock is a common symptom after an accident. Keep the dog as warm and comfortable as possible during transportation to the vet.*

initially cause no symptoms. If the dog has collapsed or cannot walk, he should be gently lifted or rolled onto a blanket which, if held at each corner, will act as a stretcher. Because the first aid advice for humans in similar situations is that they should not be moved, in case of spinal injury, people may take some persuading that the dog can be lifted. However, there are generally no roadside emergency facilities for dogs equivalent to the human ambulance, so the quickest way for an animal to receive treatment is to take it directly to a clinic.

dog fights

Dog fights can result in severe injuries to the throat or chest, particularly if a small dog is attacked by a larger one. Tissues such as muscles and blood vessels may be badly damaged, with the overlying skin showing merely small puncture wounds. This happens because the skin moves with the teeth during a bite, but less mobile underlying structures give way. Such small wounds may need to be opened in surgery to expose the damage and allow it to be repaired. Any dog that is severely shocked following a traffic accident or

fight may need intravenous fluids and drugs to help stabilize the body before a general anesthetic can be given.

gastric torsion

Gastric dilation or torsion is a condition that mainly affects large breeds. It constitutes an extreme emergency and is fatal if veterinary attention is not sought in time. Although the causes of the condition are not definitely known, it usually occurs within two hours of a meal. The stomach, having first become filled with air and gas, then twists around on its attachments in the abdomen. This results in collapse of the blood circulation and extreme shock. Death rapidly follows.

While the stomach is filling with gas, the dog will often try to vomit, though nothing is brought up. If the symptoms are noticed at this stage, veterinary treatment involves a tube being passed into the stomach to relieve the pressure. The dog's chances of survival are much greater than if the stomach has already twisted, requiring surgical emptying.

cuts and wounds

Pressure should be applied to any injury resulting in bleeding while

transport to a clinic is being arranged. The amount of blood is not necessarily proportional to the size of the wound—small punctures or cuts to a foot pad or ear can produce alarmingly copious amounts, whereas a large skin tear may result in almost no blood loss. Wrapping an injured foot in cotton batting and bandaging evenly and firmly helps to stem blood flow. A cut ear may be similarly padded and strapped to the dog's head to prevent shaking, which prolongs bleeding.

heat stroke

Hyperthermia, or heat stroke, produces devastating damage to the body and commonly affects older, overweight dogs exercising in hot weather.

Panting is the only way a dog can lose body heat. If the heart and lungs are inefficient, heat cannot be lost more quickly than it is gained so that the body temperature can rise as high as 108°F (40°C). Young, healthy dogs are also affected—sadly, many dogs are still subjected to the torture of being confined in a car in hot weather, despite much publicity. Even if the windows are left open, temperatures within the car rise dramatically and the body quickly overheats. Hosing down or immersing the dog in cold water may reduce the body temperature in time to save its life. If, however, the dog is already semi-conscious or unconscious, the chances of survival are not good.

eclampsia

Milk fever, or eclampsia, also causes an increase in body temperature associated with a fall in the levels of calcium in the blood. This occurs typically in bitches of small breeds, such as the Yorkie, in the first two weeks after giving birth. Relatively large quantities of milk are being produced at this time and, if the diet contains insufficient calcium to meet the demand, blood levels fall. The dog

may pant excessively and become wobbly on her feet. Veterinary help should be sought immediately and intravenous injections of calcium will be necessary to correct the deficiency.

insect bites and stings

Although more common during the summer, stings can occur at any time of year if a dog encounters a sleepy insect with his nose or paw. If sudden, puffy swelling of the lips and nose is seen, an allergic reaction to a sting should be suspected and the dog should be checked out as soon as possible. If you know whether a wasp or bee was responsible, vinegar can be applied to a wasp sting and bicarbonate of soda to a bee sting, to counteract the alkaline and acid nature of the stings.

The allergic reaction may be confined to the muzzle or it may spread to cause irritation and swelling in the skin over other parts of the body. As with humans, it is possible, though rare, for the reaction to become more severe with successive

above: *Heat stroke can occur in any breed of dog. Emergency treatment includes reducing body temperature with large quantities of cold water.*

stings, so always seek veterinary advice.

fits and seizures

One of the most common reasons for an anxious phone call after working hours is that the dog has collapsed and is in the process of having an epileptic fit. If this is the first fit an owner has seen, it can be an extremely alarming and upsetting event and it can be difficult to reassure them that the episode will subside in the next few minutes. Dogs that are rushed to a clinic are almost always completely normal by the time they arrive and the vet is therefore completely dependent on an accurate description of symptoms for a diagnosis of epilepsy to be made. On the rare occasions that a fit does not resolve itself, the dog will need to be taken to the clinic for the fit to be interrupted with sedative medication.

common problems

skin conditions

The most common symptom of skin trouble is itchiness, often as frustrating for the owner to watch as for the dog to experience, and many skin complaints are complicated by self-damage through excessive licking, chewing, or scratching, which can perpetuate the problem long after the original cause has disappeared. Such behavior may even become an irritating attention-seeking habit!

The most frequent culprit is the ubiquitous flea, *Ctenocephalides felis* being the most common species, which causes anything from a mild irritation and an occasional scratch behind the ear to severe and extremely distressing allergic reactions. Flea bite hypersensitivity is an allergy that develops to the saliva of the flea, introduced into the dog's skin as the flea sucks blood. Initial scabs and crusting can progress, if untreated, to extensive baldness and skin thickening. Allergic dogs may not carry many fleas themselves but react to the often unnoticed infestations carried by non-itchy animals in the same household.

Mange mites, tiny parasites related to spiders that live on or burrow into the skin, such as *Chelytiella* and *Sarcoptes*, are contagious and also cause severe skin damage. The *Demodex* mange mite, on the other hand, is carried in the hair follicles from birth, is not contagious, and typically causes baldness but no irritation.

Ear mites (*Otodectes*) are confined to the ear canal, where they cause accumulation of thick, black wax, and are frequently seen in young puppies from dubious backgrounds. Untreated infection in the mother is passed directly to the pups as soon as the ear

above: *Skin conditions are relatively common in dogs. Early treatment is always recommended.*

canal opens soon after birth. Adult dogs may pick up infection through contact with cats who, though carrying large numbers of mites, may show no symptoms of irritation or discomfort.

Both flea and mange mite infestations are frequently complicated by secondary bacterial infections, so thorough treatment involves the administration of antibiotics. Drugs are also frequently needed to control itchiness and prevent self-damage.

Other allergies also cause inflammation and swelling of the skin. The distribution of the resulting rash may give clues as to the initiating cause. Food allergies may result in small swellings all over the skin, whereas contact allergies affect the feet, lower parts of the chest and abdomen, and between the back legs.

Bacterial infections can result in

either a flaky, scurfy coat, needing regular baths with an effective medicated shampoo, or in the canine equivalent of acne, where pustules develop particularly on the muzzle and in the groin of young dogs. Scarring may ensue, despite the use of antibiotics. Certain breeds, such as the Bull Terrier and Staffordshire Terrier, are prone to abscesses between the toes (interdigital cysts), which may need lancing and treatment with long courses of antibiotics.

Changes in the skin may be associated with other systemic disease and will be taken into account when these conditions are diagnosed. Non-itchy hair loss and thinning of the skin may be part of Cushings syndrome, in which the body produces too much cortisone. Bald areas with blackened skin, clammy to the touch, may be caused by bowel tumors, where symptoms may develop slowly over a period of weeks, or by the swallowing of non-digestible objects which, if not vomited up directly, may pass into the intestine from the stomach, become lodged, and cause the sudden onset of severe vomiting. The obstruction may be able to be felt through the abdominal wall or X-rays may need to be taken for confirmation of the diagnosis. Prompt surgical attention is essential to remove the obstruction and to prevent the development of complications such as bowel perforation and peritonitis. Offending items commonly include stones and corn cobs but plastic toys out of cereal boxes, tights, and even bunches of keys occasionally crop up to make life more interesting!

pyometra

The most common condition causing persistent vomiting in the older, unspayed bitch is an infection of the womb, or pyometra. Other symptoms may include an unpleasant vaginal discharge, excessive thirst, reduced or absent appetite, and a high temperature.

The condition classically occurs within two months of a season that may have been heavier than usual, and seems to be more frequent in bitches who have suffered false pregnancies. Medical treatment may suppress the condition temporarily but a complete hysterectomy is the treatment of choice and carries a very good prognosis.

coughs

A cough is another frequently described symptom that may signal merely an infection or be indicative of more serious disease. Infectious bronchitis—formerly known as kennel cough—can often be diagnosed at a distance as the typically persistent,

hacking cough is heard from the waiting room. The dog may retch following a bout of coughing and is often thought to have something stuck in the throat. Vaccination is available against one of the main causative organisms, *Bordetella bronchiseptica*, but as many other bacteria and viruses can be involved, this is not always effective. However, the infection does not usually make the dog feel ill and in many cases responds readily to antibiotics.

A retching cough in the older dog, often worse when it is exercising or excited, may indicate heart disease. The most common form in the dog is damaged and leaky heart valves (endocardiosis), which lead to inefficient pumping action of the heart muscle and an audible heart murmur. The heart becomes dilated and weak, and fluid dams back and collects in the lungs and abdominal cavity. Diuretic drugs are used either on their own to increase fluid loss through the kidneys, thereby reducing the load on the heart, or in combination with other drugs, improving cardiac performance. Certain breeds, such as the Cavalier King Charles Spaniel, may develop heart murmurs when very young; congenital heart failure is very common in middle-aged and old dogs of this breed.

diabetes

Increase in thirst is a frequently reported symptom, again seen more commonly as dogs get older. The amount a dog drinks is closely linked to the quantity of urine produced, so an inability to get through the night without mishap may be the first sign that the water intake has increased.

Increased thirst and appetite are classic symptoms of sugar diabetes

right: An increase in water consumption may indicate an underlying clinical problem.

(*diabetes mellitus*), which is caused by a lack of insulin production from the pancreas. The function of insulin is to allow sugar into the cells, which is metabolized to release energy. In the absence of insulin, the body feels it is starving, hence the increase in appetite, and blood and urine glucose rises abnormally. Daily injections of insulin are required to replace the deficiency.

kidney disease

The function of the kidney is to eliminate waste products from the body and regulate the amount of water. As dogs age, it is common for the kidney to lose the ability to concentrate urine, resulting in increased urine production and an associated increase in thirst. As long as such dogs are free to drink what they need, the body remains in balance and the dog appears well. Any coincidental problem, however, that results in the dog drinking less than it needs or losing more fluid than it

should, such as vomiting or diarrhea, can upset this delicate balance, resulting in rapid dehydration and precipitating kidney failure. Blood tests may be necessary to determine the severity of kidney malfunction and whether the dog is likely to respond to rehydration therapy.

cystitis

Cystitis (inflammation of the bladder) is heralded by an increase in frequency of urine being passed, often accompanied by painful straining, and may be caused by bacterial infection, urinary crystals, or bladder stones, or more seriously, by cancer of the bladder. A fresh urine sample for testing is very important whenever the symptoms include any alterations in water intake or urine output and you will impress your vet enormously if you have already collected a sample in a clean container without being asked.

If a urine test is inconclusive, further examinations including X-rays may be required. A technique where the bladder is filled with air to highlight any defects or abnormalities (pneumocystogram) is particularly useful to diagnose bladder stones and tumors.

lameness

Another commonly occuring symptom is lameness, usually as a result of an injury of some sort. The severity of the limp can vary from very mild, as with a nail bed infection or pedal dermatitis, to moderate, as with a splinter or piece of glass in a pad, or can be so severe that the dog can bear no weight on the leg at all, for example if a bone in the leg is fractured.

Cruciate ligament rupture is a common injury in larger breeds that results in instability of the stifle, or knee joint, and may lead to joint degeneration and arthritis if undiagnosed. Surgical correction of the instability is frequently necessary.

Lameness that is recurrent or gets worse over a period of time may be caused by developmental problems such as *osteochondrosis dessicans* (OCD), which can affect several joints, including the shoulder, elbow, and hock. The condition occurs when splits form in the normally smooth cartilage covering the end of the bone. A flap of cartilage may then lift off the surface, causing pain when the joint moves. The symptoms may subside spontaneously if the flap becomes detached and comes to lie to one side of the joint cavity. Surgery may otherwise be required to remove the flap.

lumps

Vets are frequently consulted concerning lumps of various descriptions that can appear anywhere over the surface of the dog. Benign tumors are generally slow-growing, aren't painful, and do not spread to other parts of the body. Malignant growths, on the other hand, may be inflamed and painful, grow rapidly, and may spread through the blood or lymph circulation to grow elsewhere.

Certain benign tumors, such as fatty growths, or lipomas, can reach considerable size and may eventually interfere with limb movement. Mammary tumors are more likely to be

zoonoses

Zoonotic diseases are those that are transmissible from animals to man. Although such diseases are rare, you need to take precautions and be aware that there can be problems. Misinformation is often spread through ignorance or fear.

dog bites

Dogs carry a wide range of bacteria in their mouths, and a bite commonly results in deposition of bacteria deep beneath the surface of the skin. These bacteria may then proliferate and cause a painful swelling or even an abscess. Bite wounds should always be carefully washed, and for anything more than a small "scratch," you should seek medical attention, since a course of antibiotics may be required. Medical advice should also be sought if any swelling, pain, or obvious infection occurs.

fleas

Dogs and cats share the same species of flea, most commonly *Ctenocephalides felis*. The common fleas cannot survive on human blood, but they can bite humans and cause skin irritation. A variety of effective products are available for controlling fleas, and your veterinarian can advise you on the best products to use.

ringworm

Ringworm (dermatophytosis) is one of the most common zoonotic diseases derived from dogs. Ringworm is a fungal infection of the skin, and the most common cause is an organism called *Microsporum canis*. In humans, as with the dog, ringworm can cause patches of hair loss, but infection is more common on the arms, body, or legs, where circular patches of reddened skin are a common sign. If your dog is infected with ringworm, this can be successfully treated, but avoid excessive close contact with the dog, and wear gloves when handling, until the problem has been resolved.

It is important not to let children have direct contact with ringworm-infected pets. Ringworm in humans

benign than breast cancer in humans and often remain static for a long time. However, if malignant, they may already have spread to other parts of the body, particularly the lung, by the time the growth is noticed. A chest X ray should always be taken to try to eliminate this possibility before surgery is performed.

can also be treated successfully with a variety of drugs but medical attention is necessary if you suspect this problem. Ringworm spores are shed into the environment from infected dogs and are quite resistant. Thorough cleaning throughout the house, including regular vacuum cleaning and disinfecting where possible, is therefore recommended.

toxoplasmosis

Toxoplasmosis is a parasite that infects many mammals, including humans. It is primarily a concern for pregnant women since, if infection occurs during pregnancy, damage can occur to the developing fetus. Most human infections come from poor meat hygiene (handling uncooked meat or eating undercooked meat). However, for a short period after they are first infected with toxoplasma, dogs may shed eggs (oocysts) in their feces, and this is another potential source of infection for humans.

intestinal worms

Very rarely humans can become infected with a dog roundworm (*Toxocara canis*) or the tapeworm (*Dipylidium caninum*). Of the two, canine roundworm infections are more common in people, but regular worming of dogs for both roundworms and tapeworms is an important part of general health care.

campylobacter and salmonella

These are two intestinal bacteria that can cause severe gastrointestinal disturbances and can affect many animals, including humans. Infection in humans is usually through the food chain, and infection from dogs is rare, although they are a potential source. Routine hygiene precautions (for example, washing hands after handling a dog) should always be followed, but particular care should be paid to handling dogs with diarrhea.

If the diarrhea is prolonged, severe, or contains blood, veterinary attention should always be sought to identify the underlying cause. If campylobacter or salmonella are identified, specific treatment and/or monitoring may be required.

the **older** dog

Many conditions seen commonly in the older dog are often assumed to be "just old age." I find this a most frustrating phrase, particularly when used to describe an obviously ailing animal who has not seen the inside of a veterinary clinic for years. Certainly, problems such as arthritis, tumors, obesity, and heart or kidney disease, may be age-related and incurable. However, this does not necessarily mean that the uncomfortable effects of such conditions cannot be alleviated by owner observation and prompt veterinary care. If pain and discomfort can be relieved, we are under the same obligation to do so as in the case of a younger dog and, if we could ask many of our patients, I'm sure they would agree. Any concern about the risks of general anesthesia in the older dog is generally unfounded with the advent of extremely safe and quick-acting anesthetic agents, such as propofol and isoflurane gas, and the incidence of anesthetic-related problems is no greater than in younger animals.

Many dogs become less active as they get older and it may be assumed that putting on weight is an automatic consequence of this change in behavior. However, maintaining a dog at its correct bodyweight is the single most important factor in ensuring a comfortable old age. Fat not only accumulates where we can see, but can also exacerbate conditions such as heart, lung, and joint disease.

Several diets are now available that take the special requirements of the older dog into consideration, with reduced protein, salt, and, most important, reduced calorie content, although the bulk of

left: *Graying around the muzzle, but still alert, this older dog enjoys his "golden" years.*

the diet remains the same. If fed from an appropriate age and before symptoms of disease become obvious, body function can be maintained at the best possible levels despite inevitable age-related deterioration.

A major cause of chronic pain and discomfort in the older dog is dental disease and this can also bring human distress, due to the foul smell that accompanies it. Dental tartar can be thought of as infected mineral deposits that build up progressively if no efforts are made to keep the teeth clean. Specially formulated pastes and toothbrushes are available that considerably reduce the incidence of disease if used routinely. A bristled fingerbrush may be easier to use than a regular brush, as it is more likely to be accepted by the dog as a part of your hand.

Many old-age problems are, of course, progressive and untreatable, and, however much one may wish it, such terminal conditions make dying peacefully at home extremely unlikely. An assessment of a dog's quality of life is usually best made by those the dog lives with, although, in some cases, deterioration in physical condition may be more easily determined by the vet who does not see the dog every day. Conversely, a vet may occasionally be put under pressure to agree that euthanasia is the best option when, in fact, treatment may be feasible.

Ideally, a decision to put an old dog to sleep should be made with the informed consent of everyone involved and with concern for the animal's welfare uppermost. Although we will always grieve for a lost companion, the sadness should be accompanied by a feeling of

satisfaction and relief that the only humane course of action has been taken. Vets receive many more letters of thanks following euthanasia than after successful medical or surgical treatment, however miraculous, confirming that putting an animal to sleep in a sensitive and caring way is one of the most important, though often distressing, services that vets offer.

above: *Gentle exercise and mental stimulation is still important as the dog matures.*

above: *The Wetmararner and,* **left***, a relaxed Golden Retreiver, are two distinctive, and very different looking, members of the gundog breeds.*

The variety of appearance
and function of dog breeds
is immense. From
Chihuahua to Great Dane,
each breed has its specific
characteristics and
behaviors, yet they all
belong to the same species.

dog
breeds

introduction
to breed section

There are literally hundreds of breeds of dog in the world, ranging from the giants, such as the Great Dane and the Mastiff, to the diminutive Yorkshire Terrier and Chihuahua. In most cases, the size and overall appearance of the dog reflects the task that it was bred for; only in recent years have people bred dogs purely for the way they look.

Although most of us are attracted to a breed by its appearance, selection should always take into account behavior, exercise needs, and breed characteristics, as well as grooming requirements.

Any dog is only what you make it, however, so early socialization and training is a must, no matter what the breed.

hereditary diseases

A hereditary disease is one that is passed from parent to offspring as a result of the animal's genetic make-up. Breed-related problems are those that occur more commonly in certain breeds. They may be hereditary in nature or merely associated with breeds

above: *A Bullmastiff showing heavy facial wrinkling—a result of selective breeding.*

below: *A product of man's intervention, the Lowchen, or "Little Lion Dog," is trimmed according to tradition.*

that have a similar size or conformation. Both hereditary and breed-related problems can occur at any time during the life of the dog. Congenital abnormalities are specifically those that are present at birth, and they can include hereditary or breed-related conditions. They may also be the result of a spontaneous mutation of the genetic code or a defect in the embryo's development in the womb.

As awareness of the genetic basis of many breed-related diseases increase, programs to screen and prevent breeding affected animals can be put in place in an attempt to reduce incidence of disease. Hip dysplasia is a hereditary condition characterized by abnormal development of the hip joint. The condition can cause pain and disability in the young dog or severe arthritis later in life. Progressive Retinal Atrophy (PRA) involves thinning of the retina at the back of the eye, gradual loss of its blood supply, and eventual blindness. Both conditions are being monitored to discourage breeding affected dogs.

Another unfortunate condition is heart valve abnormality, which affects breeds including the Cavalier King Charles Spaniel. These abnormalities are often undetectable until a litter has been bred from the animal, or they may become evident in a very young dog.

Other hereditary eye conditions include: cataracts, a defect of the lens of the eye resulting in opacity and blindness; micropthalmos, an abnormally small eye inherited particularly in Dobermans and Collie breeds; entropion and ectropion, defects where the eyelids roll in or out respectively and need surgical correction; and distichiasis, an uncomfortable condition where extra rows of eyelashes grow and rub on the surface of the eye.

Hemophilia and von Willebrand's disease are both caused by hereditary deficiencies of blood clotting factors and result in spontaneous and life-threatening bleeding into body tissues. They are both sex-linked, affecting only male dogs, though the relevant gene is carried by the female to be passed on to her offspring. Hemophilia is seen in most breeds, whereas von Willebrand's disease has been identified in only seven breeds, including Scotties, Dobermans, and German Shepherd Dogs.

Patella luxation, or displacement of the kneecap, is a hereditary condition seen in toy and small breeds, such as the Yorkshire Terrier and Westie, and may require surgery to hold the patella in place. Legge-Perthes disease, which results in a defect of blood supply to the head of the femur and its subsequent painful degeneration, is seen commonly in young animals of the same breeds.

Dermoid sinus, or cyst, is a rare condition usually seen only in the Rhodesian Ridgeback but very occasionally in other breeds. A defect during the development of the embryo results in the hair-covered skin remaining connected with the outer layers of the spinal cord.

Scottie cramp is thought to be a neurological condition where the animal collapses without loss of consciousness, following exercise or excitement. Its cause is unknown, and though first seen in young Scottish Terriers, it has also been recognized in other terrier breeds.

below: *A West Highland White Terrier prone to a number of hereditary diseases.*

ancient breeds

left: *The elegant Basenji. This breed "sings" rather than barks.*

Canaan Dog

height *large (19–24 inches/48–61 centimeters)*
breed needs *Somewhat aloof and self-occupied, the breed can make a good companion if socialized early with humans and other dogs.*

The national dog of Israel, this compact, spitz-type dog is nearly always sandy in color, although white, brown, and black are permissible. Originally a pariah, living off the waste of human encampments, today the breed is trainable and versatile.

Dingo

height *large (21 inches/53 centimeters)*
breed needs *As one of the few groups of free-living dogs in the world, the basic nature of the Dingo makes them fascinating to observe, but unsuitable as pets. A license is required to own one.*

below: *Thr Canaan Hound: an ancient breed still kept as a companion today.*

Basenji

height *medium
(16–17 inches/40.5–43 centimeters)*
breed needs *This is an independent dog, although affable and content to have human company. Extensive and early socialization with people is necessary, and recall training essential if the Basenji is not to wander.*
hereditary problems *Eye testing required.*

An ancient breed, the Basenji has all the appearance of a desert dweller. Compact and agile, with large upright ears and a charmingly wrinkled expression, these dogs are nearly always sandy-white in color. Unlike most dogs, they do not bark, but give an amazing "yodel." Like the wolf, females come into season only once a year, and males are able to retract their testicles until breeding occurs.

The only true "domestic" dog to live a completely feral existence, the Dingo can be regarded as semi-wild. Living in large groups in its native Australia, where it arrived over 4,000 years ago, it has settled successfully, without human interference. Kept occasionally as pets and alarm raisers by the Aborigines, they are regarded as pests by many, and have only recently been legally accepted as pets in domestic homes.

Ibizan Hound

height *large (22–29 inches/56–73.5 centimeters)*
breed needs *Quiet and affectionate in the home, yet racy and active outside, Ibizan Hounds are relatively unchanged and unspoiled by intensive breeding. Not dogs to live outdoors, Ibizan Hounds feel the cold and prefer the luxuries of the living room.*

With a clean, elegant outline and huge upright ears, the Ibizan Hound seems to match the image of a reclining sphinx. Used for hare and rabbit coursing, this breed hunts by sight, sound, and smell and can cover ground and turn like a Greyhound.

Mexican Hairless Dog

height *medium
(16–22 inches/40.5–56 centimeters)*
breed needs *Although these dogs appear to be delicate, they are robust and tenacious characters, needing early and ongoing socialization, particularly with children. Their skin also needs daily attention to remain in good condition.*

Notable for its total lack of hair, the Mexican Hairless Dog, or Xoloitzcuintli, is small and almost terrier-like in conformation. The naked appearance of these dogs is carried on a recessive gene, meaning that some dogs in each litter are born with hair. These are called "powder-puffs," and although they are not suitable for showing, they are essential for breeding purposes, as hairless mated to hairless would eventually mean the extinction of the breed.

New Guinea Singing Dog

height *medium
(14–15 inches/35.5–38 centimeters)*
breed needs *Rare and exotic, this breed is definitely not a pet. It is shy and aloof, although it will tolerate proximity to people.*

The New Guinea Singing Dog is so-called due to its unique melodious voice. Nearly lost as a pure breed in the 1960s, two pairs of wild dogs were eventually captured in New Guinea and bred as zoo animals until numbers increased. Several of these ancient pariahs still live in zoos across the world. Numbers living in the wild are unknown.

gundogs

Spaniels. The Field Spaniel is less popular in number and is rarely seen outside working homes. Their long, lean heads and glossy, silky coats, which can be black, liver, or roan, make them a distinctive dog.

Clumber Spaniels are the true heavyweights of this group. Weighing in at 80 pounds (36.3 kg) or even more, they are stoic workers, with a good hunting drive to follow scent. They are equally happy at home, snoring in their basket. The Sussex is also a massively boned dog, and can be noisy when out exercising and following a scent.

Cocker Spaniel/
American Cocker Spaniel

height *medium (Cocker: 15–16 ins; 38–40.5 cm American Cocker: 14–15 ins; 35.5–40.5 cm)*

breed needs *A "busy" dog, this breed may become "self-employed" if left to its own devices. They need companionship and mental stimulation. Even the longer-coated American Cocker is built to work, and although hampered by the "show" coat, is more than happy to dispense with it as a family pet.*

hereditary problems *Hip dysplasia, eye defects, and some kidney defects are problems in these breeds. Some behavioral problems have been linked to the solid-color Cockers, particularly gold.*

It's no wonder that this spaniel is often referred to as the "merry Cocker"— their tails never stop wagging! Cocker Spaniels could be regarded as the Border Collie of the gundog world— medium-sized they may be, but their hearts belong to the fields. A true working dog, Cockers are adaptable enough to learn any new skill, if trained gently, then master it.

Chesapeake Bay Retriever

height *large (21–26 ins; 53.5–66 cm)*

breed needs *Sufficient exercise and the opportunity to put swimming skills to good use are a priority with this dog. Chesapeakes are responsive to careful training and handling. They make excellent, sensible companions, although they can be independent.*

hereditary problems *Breeding stock should be eye-tested.*

A powerful, compact breed, this is a dog designed to retrieve ducks and waterfowl from the icy waters off the shores of the Chesapeake Bay. This dog's thick coat has a soft wooly layer close to the skin for warmth and a harsh, oily layer of coarse hair on the outside to repel water.

Clumber Spaniel/
Sussex Spaniel/Field Spaniel

height *medium (Clumber: 19–20 ins; 48–51 cm Sussex: 15–16 ins; 38–40.5 cm Field: 20–23 ins; 51–58.5 cm)*

breed needs *Field Spaniels are highly active working dogs, constantly on the go. Clumbers and Sussex Spaniels, on the other hand, enjoy their home comforts as well as their outdoor excursions, and should not be over-exercised while young nor allowed to become overweight in later life.*

hereditary problems *Clumber Spaniels and Sussex Spaniels have a high incidence of hip dysplasia. Field Spaniels should also be tested before breeding.*

The heavier end of the Spaniel set includes the Clumber and Sussex

top: Water lover—the noble profile of a Chesapeake Bay Retriever.

left: The rare Field Spaniel and, right, his heavyweight cousin, the Clumber.

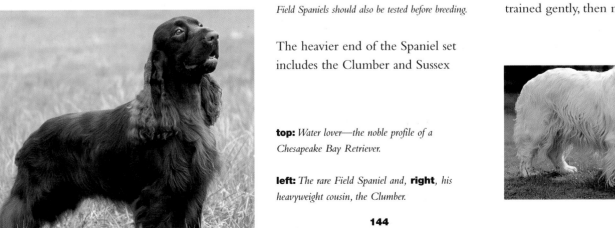

Curly Coated Retriever

height *large (25–27 ins; 63.5–68.5 cm)*

breed needs *A truly ancient breed, with no known hereditary problems or behavioral anomalies. The coat needs some care to maintain water-repelling properties.*

As the name suggests, this is a dog with an amazing curly coat. Only the face and muzzle are curl-free, as the rest makes perfect water-proofing. A real outdoor type, the Curly Coat is in his element retrieving birds from water, with endurance and stamina to outlast any owner. With a confident character, this is a biddable dog that responds well to training.

left: *A large personality in a small frame—the Cocker Spaniel.*

English Springer Spaniel/ Welsh Springer Spaniel/ German Spaniel/Brittany

height *medium*

(English Springer: 19–20 ins; 48–51 cm

Welsh Springer: 18–19 ins; 46–48 cm

German Spaniel: 16–20 ins; 40.5–51 cm

Brittany: 18–20.5 ins; 46–52 cm)

breed needs *All four of these breeds are highly active working dogs. Left alone for long periods of time, they can become destructive and vocal. Early training to teach them to cope without their owner for short periods is essential. Springers have been known to leap through the glass panes of upstairs windows in order to follow their family.*

hereditary problems *Hips and eyes should be tested in breeding stock.*

A true medium-sized dog, the Springer is a versatile gundog, working dog, or pet. Said to be the oldest of sporting gundogs, this breed was designed to flush out game birds, so that they "spring" upward.

The appearance of the working and show types are now divergent—the show types being heavier, with deeper heads and more feathering overall. The Welsh Springer is even more distinctive in appearance—his coat being a delicious combination of dark red and white patches.

The German Spaniel is rarely seen outside its native country, and even there is primarily a working gundog. Of similar size and appearance to the working English Springer, this is a specialist owner's breed only!

The Brittany is also a tireless worker. The most popular native breed in France, this dog makes an excellent companion and gundog, with good retrieving ability. The distinctive stumpy tail is a feature of this breed.

Golden Retriever/ Flat-coated Retriever

height *large (20–24 ins; 51–61 cm)*

breed needs *Substantial amounts of mental and physical exercise. Regular grooming required or your carpets will take on a golden hue! Some males can be stubborn and all Goldens need careful and sensitive training.*

hereditary problems *Hips and eyes should be tested in breeding stock.*

Known as an excellent all-around dog, the Golden Retriever has been

above: *A true working dog, the Brittany needs plenty of exercise and training.*

bottom: *Golden Retrievers are among the most popular pets as well as being diligent workers.*

extensively used as a guide dog, a working dog, and a wonderful family pet. Goldens have a sense of humor, which they need to share—a bored or lonely Golden will easily get into mischief.

A true working gundog, this Retriever was bred to pick up and retrieve game in the shooting field. He loves water and his coat doesn't stay golden and gleaming for long once outdoors.

The Flat-coated Retriever is equally as extroverted and cheerful as the Golden, although may retain even more working drive and ability.

Hungarian Vizsla
(smooth and wirehair)

height *large (22.5–25 ins; 57–63.5 cm)*

breed needs *Vizslas accept gentle training exceptionally well and can become quiet and sensible family pets. Without such training they can rewrite your schedule and decide their own destiny!*

hereditary problems *Hip and eye testing in breeding stock is a sensible precaution.*

A simply stunning dog from Hungary, Vizslas are immediately recognized by their distinctive russet-gold coat. This breed has a rather superior air, which matches their elegance and grace when moving. Quick to learn, Vizslas need to see the point of the task before embarking upon it. They are lively and need sensitive early training.

Irish Water Spaniel/Barbet

height *large (20–23 ins; 51–58.5 cm)*

breed needs *Ideal as a country walking companion, both breeds need extensive exercise to remain in peak physical and mental states.*

hereditary problems *Hips and eyes should be tested in breeding stock. Some hip dysplasia, but otherwise a healthy breed.*

above: *A smooth-haired Hungarian Vizsla radiates elegance and working ability.*

left: *A dog in sheep's clothing—the Irish Water Spaniel.*

As its name implies, the Irish Water Spaniel is a true water dog—covered in tight chocolate-brown curls of hair, with a top knot to cover its eyes in rough cover. The breed is thought to have originated in Ireland in the 1800s. Despite its extensive retrieving abilities, it has never been popular as a pet. The Barbet has a similar coat and

above: *Almost extinct after World War II, Dutch enthusiasts have saved the Kooikerhondje.*

retrieving drive, but is thought to have originated in France.

Italian Spinone/
Bracco Italiano

height *large (24–26 ins; 61–66 cm)/ Bracco Italiano large (24–26.5 ins; 61–67 cm)*

breed needs *Once fully grown, this breed needs above-average amounts of exercise. Their coats are remarkably easy to care for—shedding dirt and grime once dry, although with the potential to carry odors longer. The Bracco Italiano is similar in nature, although with a smooth-coated appearance.*

hereditary problems *Spinones' hips and eyes need testing. All Bracco parents should be tested for hip dysplasia; some elbow problems.*

A hardy worker, these breeds are perfectly designed for hunting through heavy cover in the field, but are equally suited to lounging on the couch! A stable character that responds well to early, gentle training, the Spinone will offer loyalty and companionship, while resting his well-whiskered chin on your knee (but watch out for slobber!).

left: *Lying down on the job—the Italian Spinone is supposed to be a hard worker…*

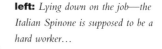

Kooikerhondje

height *medium (14–16 ins; 35.5–40.5 cm)*

breed needs *The silky, attractive coat of the Kooikerhondje requires regular grooming to keep it knot-free. The ideal size and calm character of this dog make it suitable for all environments as a family pet. Sensitive, gentle training required.*

hereditary problems *Hips and eyes should be tested in breeding stock. Screening for von Willebrand's disease recommended.*

An ancient breed, originating from the Netherlands in the 1700s, this medium-sized dog was bred to entice ducks off the lake and into the hunters' nets by acting as a decoy. After World War II, only 25 Kooikerhondje were known to exist, but breed enthusiasts have now secured the future of these delightful and attractive dogs.

Labrador Retriever

height *large (21.5–22.5 ins; 55–57 cm)*

breed needs *Labradors are inclined to chew and can be extremely bouncy when young, but plenty of exercise keeps them out of trouble. Early training and company are also important.*

hereditary problems *Hips and eyes should be tested in breeding stock. Hip dysplasia, elbow problems, and eye defects are all prevalent in the breed.*

The ultimate "wash and wear" working gundog, the Labrador's enthusiasm for life is equaled by a passion for food.

above: *The large Munsterlander—a tireless worker that needs an experienced handler.*

It is thought that the Labrador was first bred by fishermen off the coast of Newfoundland, where they were required to plunge into icy water to retrieve fishing nets—they still love water today.

Large Munsterlander/ Small Munsterlander

height *large (23–24 ins; 58.5–61 cm), medium (19–22 ins; 48–56 cm)*

breed needs *Exercise is a must with this breed. Even the smaller version needs to expend energy by running free—and it is a joy to watch it doing so.*

hereditary problems *Hips and eyes should be tested in breeding stock. Hip dysplasia and elbow problems ensure the need for screening.*

Another all-around dog, from Munster in Germany, this hunt, point, retrieve breed may look like a giant Border Collie to the uninitiated, but has a real sense of purpose all of its own. He has a strong desire to hunt, and needs careful training to guard against "selective deafness." This dog has a silky black-and-white coat, with abundant feathering and a long, plumed tail.

left: *Treasured as gundogs, guide dogs, and pets, Labradors are assured their place as true all-around dogs.*

Nova Scotia Duck Tolling Retriever

height *medium (17–21 ins; 43–53.5 cm)*
breed needs *This is an intelligent and fast-moving dog, which can be equally well taught to frolic in the obedience ring or working trial competition.*
hereditary problems *Hips and eyes should be tested in breeding stock.*

A gundog with a remarkable name and an unforgettable history. Bred by Canadian hunters, the dog is said to frolic on the shore, to entice curious ducks and geese to come within firing range. The dog then acts as an efficient retriever. A true medium size, the Nova Scotia Duck Tolling Retriever is deep red in color, with a well-feathered, luxurious coat.

above left: *A truly medium-sized gundog, the Novia Scotia Duck Tolling Retriever.*

above: *The English Pointer.*

Picardy Spaniel

height *large (22–24 ins; 56–61 cm)*
breed needs *A rare breed, with no known hereditary problems. Gentle and sensitive, this dog needs training to match.*

An unusual sight outside its native France, this large spaniel (not pictured) was originally bred to find and retrieve game birds and waterfowl. It loves water and works with stamina and endurance. Despite its size and energy, the Picardy is a calm and sensible house dog that loves companionship and affection.

Pointers—English, German Shorthair, Wirehair

height *large (24–26 ins; 61–66 cm)*
breed needs *Exercise is a must with these breeds. Even the graceful English Pointer needs to let off steam and engage in some "hunt, point, retrieve" behaviors from time to time. Coats are generally easy-care, being either short and coarse or, in the case of the German Wirehaired Pointer, harsh and wiry.*

The most elegant of the gundogs, Pointers were originally bred to indicate fallen game, as well as to hunt and retrieve. Their energy and stamina make them excellent working dogs, and wonderful pets for those who live an outdoor life and enjoy all weather.

left: *The German Wirehair Pointer showing the heavy whiskers distinctive of the breed.*

Portuguese Water Dog

height *medium (17–22 ins; 43–56 cm)*

breed needs *The Portuguese Water Dog is traditionally clipped over the rear end, presumably to assist swimming, while the tail is left with a distinctive plume. This clip is accepted for both working and showing. A rather reserved character, this breed requires more than the usual amount of socialization with people while young.*

An ancient breed, the Portuguese Water Dog is thought to have first arrived in Portugal in the Middle Ages. It is an adaptable dog, strong, and fearless, and has been used to help haul in fishing nets and as a vermin hunter. Legends also claim that this dog was used to carry messages between fishermen, by swimming from one boat to another.

Setters—Irish/ English/ Gordon/Irish Red and White

height *large (24–27 ins; 61–68.5 cm)*

breed needs *All Setters are sensitive characters that need calm, gentle training. Polite and loving house pets, they belie their appearance when in the home. Setters have fine, wavy coats that need regular grooming but little bathing.*

hereditary problems *Hips and eyes should be tested in breeding stock. Hip dysplasia can be a problem in English, Irish, and Gordon Setters. Eye-testing is advisable in Irish and Irish Red and Whites.*

right: *Extroverted and loving, all the Setters make amiable pets, given sensitive training.*

above: *The "Silver Shadows" of the dog world— a pair of stunning Weimaraners.*

left: *The unusual Portuguese Water Dog.*

All the Setters are excellent hunters, bred to locate game in the shooting field. Each variation has its own distinct personality: the Irish, Gordon, and Irish Red and White are all extroverted, happy-go-lucky, and enjoy a frolic—sometimes to the point of being scatterbrained. The English is perhaps more sensible, but may still get carried away with scents from the grass and ignore their master when called.

Weimaraner (smooth and long-coat)

height *large (22–27 ins; 56–68.5 cm)*

breed needs *A dog for the experienced owner. Males need extra socialization with other dogs when young, and all require good exercise and sensible training. Weimaraners have been used as police dogs and drug detection dogs, but in the wrong hands can be powerful and strong willed.*

hereditary problems *No major health problems, although hip screening is sensible.*

A true hunt, point, retrieve breed from Germany, the Weimaraner has enjoyed increased popularity in the last decade. This dog possesses a stunning "silver" coat—as well as great stature and a noble head, with pale eyes. The long-coated variety has silky hair up to 2 inches (5 cm) in length.

sight hounds

Afghan Hound

height *large (25–29 ins; 63.5–73.5 cm)*

breed needs *Certainly, the view of the Afghan Hound's locks flowing in the wind as it gallops at high speed makes it a beautiful sight, but these dogs tend to want to run in the opposite direction from their owners if not given extensive recall training. Reserved by nature, they also need substantial socialization with people from an early age to build confidence.*

Probably the best known of all the sight hounds, the Afghan Hound is still capable of its original function today in its homeland of Afghanistan, where it is kept to hunt foxes and wolves. Its long, flowing coat almost reaches the ground, while its narrow head and triangular eyes give the dog an almost Oriental appearance.

Borzoi

height *large (27–31 ins; 68.5–78.5 cm)*

breed needs *Regular grooming, sensitive companionship, and early recall training are all required to keep this wonderful, gentle breed.*

Originally used as protection against wolves in their native Russia, Borzois are fast and courageous. Standing up to 31 inches (78.5 cm) at the shoulder, they are the picture of height and elegance, framed by a silky coat and wispy feathering. Now kept solely as companions, they make calm and loving pets.

Deerhound

height *large (28–30 ins; 71–76 cm)*

breed needs *Active but calm when necessary, the Deerhound offers the best of both worlds for those who can offer sufficient space to this magnificent dog. When walking outside, the strong chase instinct of all the sight hounds may come to the fore, making recall training essential.*

hereditary problems *Puppies should be liver-shunt tested.*

Wiry-coated like the Wolfhound, but with a greater turn of speed and more athletic body, this breed was originally used to hunt deer in the highlands of Scotland. Tall and elegant, this is an amenable dog, without an enemy in the world.

above right: *Aloof, but loyal to their owners, Afghan Hounds need considerable grooming.*

right: *Pets of the Russian nobility, Borzois have retained their regal appearance.*

Greyhound/Whippet/Lurcher

height *Greyhound large (27–30 ins; 68.5–76 cm),
Whippet medium (17–20 ins; 43–51 cm),
Lurcher variable (but usually over 24 ins; 61 cm.)*

breed needs *Despite their great turn of speed
outside when off the leash, Greyhounds and Whippets
usually make the most charming, quiet companions in
the home. They are renowned for their gentleness with
children and need surprisingly little exercise. They do,
however, have a tendency to chase small animals,
making early socialization with other pets essential.*

Elegant and streamlined, the
Greyhound, its smaller relative the
Whippet, and the Lurcher—a deliberate
first cross between a Greyhound and
either a terrier or collie—are designed
for speed. Greyhounds have been used
for coursing—chasing prey animals—
for centuries, and indeed, many claim
that they are one of the oldest breeds in
existence. The smooth, fine coats of
these breeds are silky to the touch and
need very little grooming. It does mean,
however, that they suffer in cold
weather.

Irish Wolfhound

height *giant (28–35 ins; 71–89 cm)*

breed needs *A gentle companion, the Irish
Wolfhound has much to recommend it. Quiet in the
home, this dog can put up a brave show as the ultimate
guard dog—simply by standing up! This breed needs
surprisingly little exercise, but a lot of leg room!*

With its height, the Irish Wolfhound
would once have been a formidable
adversary. Bred to hunt wolves, a deep
chest and long legs were required to

chase and bring them down, while an
amiable disposition ensured that they
lived as part of the family at other
times. The grizzled gray coat is highly
distinctive of this giant among breeds.

Saluki

height *large (22–28 ins; 56–71 cm)*

breed needs *Although they may appear delicate,
Salukis are quite robust and enjoy free-running.
Early socialization with dogs is a must.*

Possibly the oldest true "breed" of dog
still in existence (not pictured), the
Saluki's long history is a colorful one.
Originally used to hunt gazelles, today
it still closely resembles dogs depicted
in the tombs of Egyptian pharaohs. Its
coat is perfectly adapted for living in
desert heat—short and smooth on the
body, with long feathering on ears,
tail, and feet to protect it from the
sun.

Sloughi

height *large (24–28 ins; 61–71 cm)*

breed needs *A self-contained personality, this
breed needs extensive handling and socialization
with people if it is to overcome natural shyness.
Prefers a calm and quiet environment.*

Another ancient breed, the Sloughi
(not pictured) is still rare in countries

above: *A Greyhound, like its cousin the Lurcher,*
bottom left, *is clearly built for speed.*

outside North Africa. Perfectly colored
to blend in with sand, only the face is
marked with a darker mask. Long and
lean, this dog is aerodynamically built
for speed, and with large, doe-eyes set
in a long, expressive face, is certainly a
beautiful sight.

below: *A giant among breeds—the grizzled Irish
Wolfhound.*

scent hounds

above: *Compact and friendly, the Beagle retains strong hunting drives.*

Basset Fauve de Bretagne/ Griffon Fauve de Bretagne

height *Basset Fauve, medium (13–15 ins; 33–38 cm), Griffon Fauve, large (19–22 ins; 48–56 cm)*
breed needs *Lively and friendly, this dog wants to be where the action is. Early socialization and training are essential.*

Originally from France, the Basset Fauve de Bretagne and its larger cousin, the Griffon Fauve de Bretagne (neither pictured), is a striking and compact breed. Powerfully built to cover ground at speed while tracking a scent, this hound retains many basic characteristics and the drive to hunt. The deep golden or red coat is harsh and wiry, to protect the dog from all weather.

Basset Hound

height *medium (13–15 ins; 33–38 cm)*
breed needs *A dog with a distinct sense of humor, Bassets need companionship and mental stimulation, as well as adequate, although not excessive, exercise. Their pack hunting ancestry can make them independent and "selectively deaf" when out on walks.*
hereditary problems *Parents should be eye-tested.*

Originally an excellent hunting dog, the Basset Hound retains incredible scenting and tracking abilities. More recently, however, extremes in breeding for wrinkles, heavy bone, and size have affected the breed considerably, making it ponderous. Possibly descended from "dwarf" Bloodhounds, the Basset possesses similar loose skin on the head and neck, and remarkably long ears. A faithful and friendly dog, the Basset's booming bark is more often heard in greeting than challenge.

right: *The Basset Hound, of soulful countenance....*

Beagle

height *medium (13–16 ins; 33–40.5 cm)*
breed needs *This breed loves companionship and home comforts, but in common with all the hounds, can be an escape artist if tempted to the other side of the fence. An independent character, the Beagle needs high motivation in training or you will be left walking by yourself.*
hereditary problems *Hips and eyes need checking in breeding stock.*

A real medium-sized dog, well balanced and compact, the Beagle has been popular with hunters and families for many centuries. Originally bred for

rabbit and hare hunting, Beagles were kept in packs, but were equally content to work on their own. They have a melodious baying bark when on the scent of exciting quarry, but are affable and quiet in the home.

Bloodhounds

height *large (23–27 ins; 58.5–68.5 cm)*
breed needs *Bloodhounds are friendly and faithful—more likely to lick their quarry to death at the end of a hunt than do it harm! However, their brains are firmly directed by their noses, making positive training and a commitment to recall work essential for the family pet.*
hereditary problems *Some eye defects. Gastric torsion is a risk.*

A massive head and droopy jowls make the Bloodhound one of the most recognizable of scent hounds. This dog has a short, well-fitting coat on body and back, with a heavily wrinkled face and neck, giving a somewhat doleful appearance. An ancient breed, first recorded in the Middle Ages in Belgium and Britain, this is a dog driven by his nose. The breed's incredible scenting and tracking abilities have been used to hunt animals, and in urban searches for drugs, lost people, and even bodies. One or two packs of Bloodhounds are still kept in Britain for hunting—a rag soaked in aniseed is dragged along a track for the hounds to follow, baying as they go.

Coonhounds—Black-and-Tan/ Bluetick/English/Redbone

height *large (20–27 ins; 51–68.5 cm)*
breed needs *Calm and gentle dogs in the home if socialized and raised as family members, this breed has retained great popularity in the United States, where its prowess as a hunter is still tested at licensed trials.*

Several varieties of Coonhound exist— all primarily in the United States. Variations between the types tend to be in color and markings, while the overall strength and shape of the dog is similar. This powerful but affable breed was selectively bred to hunt and chase raccoons, finally "treeing" them and waiting underneath for the hunter to arrive. In order to alert the hunter to the cornered quarry, the Coonhound possesses a distinctive and specialized bay.

top: *A specialist tracking dog, the unmistakable Bloodhound.*

left: *A Black-and-Tan Coonhound.*

Dachshunds—standards/miniatures/smooth-haired/wirehaired/longhaired

height *small (5–10 ins; 13–26 cm)*

breed needs *As a small breed, and with a working dog's drive, Dachshunds need extra socialization when young to encourage friendly behavior with children and to learn to interact with other dogs.*

hereditary problems *All Dachshunds have the propensity for back problems.*

There are six varieties of Dachshund: Miniature longhaired, Miniature smooth-haired, Miniature wirehaired, and Standard longhaired, Standard smooth-haired, Standard wirehaired.

The word "Dachshund" means "badger dog"—aptly describing these feisty little dogs' original purpose. Indeed, the Standard sizes are still used to go to earth to hunt badgers in their native Germany, while the smaller size is ideally suited to following rabbits into their warrens. In most other countries, Dachshunds are now kept purely as companions, but they still have the ability to disappear down interesting holes after potential quarry when out for a Sunday stroll.

above right: *The Fox Hound, descended from medieval hunters.*

right: *A lively Miniature Longhaired Dachshund.*

English Fox Hound

height *large (23–27 ins; 58.5–68.5 cm)*

breed needs *Fast and athletic, a solo Foxhound will think nothing of clearing a six-foot fence to find company or quarry. These dogs need canine companionship, early and extensive training, and good control around smaller animals, which they seem driven to chase. For the experienced owner only.*

Although originating in England during the 1400s, when the fashion for fox hunting became popular, this breed undoubtedly has French ancestors. Unsuitable as a solo pet, these dogs work superbly as a team, tracking the scent of quarry and moving as a single unit until it is found. Their smooth bi-color or tri-color coats and noble head shape make them an attractive breed.

Grand Bleu de Gascoigne/Petit

height *Grand large (24–28 ins; 61–71 cm), Petit large (20–23 ins; 51–58.5 cm)*

breed needs *For experienced owners only, these large hounds need space, time, and training, as well as the opportunity to track for a living.*

Although originating from France, this dog is now more popular in the United States, where its distinctive "dappled" coat has made a mark. Bred to hunt wild boar and even wolves, the pace of this dog's tracking is not fast, but its stamina is exceptional. Closely related, the Petit version, despite its name, is not petite at all.

Hamiltonstovare

height *large (20–24 ins; 51–61 cm)*

breed needs *Fifty-nine pounds (27 kg) of pure power needs careful harnessing through sensible training. This is a hound through and through, making early socialization with small animals such as cats and small dogs essential. These dogs are generally good natured but strong-willed, making them more suitable for the experienced owner.*

A stunningly good-looking dog, the Hamiltonstovare is popular in its home country of Sweden, both as a pet and working animal. This dog is a solo hunter, with great ability to track and flush quarry, as well as alerting the hunter to the find with a great baying bark. Independent and full of energy, this distinctive tri-colored dog needs plenty of work to do if it is not to become "self-employed."

Petit Basset Griffon Vendeen/Grand Basset Griffon Vendeen

height *Petit medium (13–15 ins; 33–38 cm); Grand medium (15–16 ins; 38–40.5 cm)*

breed needs *These dogs love to run in the countryside, and need considerable training to allow it. Coat care is important.*

hereditary problems *Possible eye and back problems in the Petit Basset.*

Possessing all the charm of the Basset Hound, without excessive wrinkling or heaviness, and with a short, shaggy, and

above: *The charm of a Basset without the wrinkling—a Basset Griffon Vendeen.*

above left: *The distinctive Hamiltonstovare.*

attractive coat, the Petit Basset and the larger Grand Basset Griffon Vendeen are starting to make their mark in many European countries as a delightful pet. Originally bred to course hare, they remain determined to follow scent.

Otterhound

height *large (23–27 ins; 58.5–68.5 cm)*

breed needs *A true hound by nature, this friendly dog needs ongoing and sensitive training if its independence is to be overcome.*

hereditary problems *Hip dysplasia can be a serious problem.*

The rough, shaggy coat of the Otterhound (not pictured) was designed to protect it from the cold water on its hunt for otters. Now bred as a companion dog only, this breed still engages in water hunting activities when it gets the opportunity.

left: *A Wirehaired Dachshund.*

terriers

above: *Vermin watch out—the Australian Terrier.*

As a result of several fatal attacks on other dogs and human beings, the Pit Bull is banned in some Scandinavian countries and parts of the United States.

Airedale Terrier

height *large (22–24 ins; 56–61 cm)*
breed needs *Grooming is minimal, but its coat is shed twice a year, requiring professional stripping. This dog is courageous and determined. He needs plenty of exercise, and can be aggressive with other dogs if not well socialized from an early age.*
hereditary problems *Some hip dysplasia.*

Known as the "King of Terriers," the Airedale is truly a handsome dog. Originally bred in Yorkshire, England, this dog was designed to assist with otter and badger hunting. The dense, wiry coat is virtually waterproof and the body shape designed for strength and endurance.

American Pit Bull Terrier

height *large (18–22 ins; 46–56 cm)*
breed needs *Pit Bull Terriers need to be neutered, muzzled, and on a leash when in public in many countries. Despite these restrictions, they can be loyal and loving family pets, and are responsive to early training.*

top: *Kings of the dales, two Airedale Terriers in fine condition.*

left: *Usually outgoing and friendly, the Pit Bull Terrier has received much bad press.*

Australian Terrier

height *small (10 ins; 25.5 cm)*
breed needs *Exercise, grooming, and early handling are all required. This is an intelligent little dog with a propensity to work.*

A distant relative of the Yorkshire Terrier, now placed in the Toy group, the Australian Terrier is larger and more robust, but with the same sparkle. Bred as a farm dog in Australia, the breed's drive to catch vermin was created through combining the Cairn Terrier, Yorkshire Terrier, and the Skye Terrier.

Bedlington Terrier

height *medium (15–17 ins; 38–43 cm)*
breed needs *A bright dog, Bedlingtons need some kind of work to do to keep them occupied. Friendly and affectionate, they take well to training and are extremely agile.*
hereditary problems *Some eye defects and liver problems.*

The dog that looks like a lamb! The Bedlington Terrier is anything but lamb-like in behavior. Built to catch rabbits and vermin, this is a true terrier. The coat has a unique "linty" texture and requires little in the way of care beyond regular grooming.

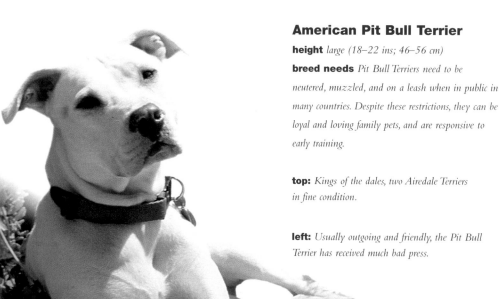

above: *Cheerful and friendly, the Border Terrier has remained a favorite family pet for hundreds of years.*

Border Terrier

height *medium (10–11 ins; 25.5–28 cm)*

breed needs *Exercise is a must for this tenacious terrier. Early socialization with other dogs, particularly for males, is also vital. Highly responsive to positive and motivational training.*

hereditary problems *Occasional back problems.*

Dating back to the 1700s, the Border Terrier has changed little in its appearance or behavior. A compact, medium-sized dog, with the stamina to keep up with a hunting party all day and the tenacity to go to earth

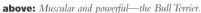

above: *Muscular and powerful—the Bull Terrier.*

after a fox, its cheerful and friendly temper make it ideally suited as a family pet.

Bull Terrier (Miniature Bull Terrier)

height *large (21–22 ins; 53.5–56 cm), Miniature small (10–14 ins; 25.5–35.5 cm)*

breed needs *Very early, extensive socialization with other dogs required. Dogs tend to be more challenging than bitches.*

hereditary problems *Some deafness. Epilepsy and related behavior problems.*

With its square, powerful build, and almost triangular head, the Bull Terrier looks every inch a fighting machine. Bred for the dog-fighting ring in the 1800s, this breed is either passionately loved or hated. Usually perfect with people and a loving family member, Bull Terriers have a personality and sense of humor all their own. Sadly this does not often extend to other dogs.

left: *The Bedlington Terrier may look as docile as a lamb, but it is a typical terrier in behavior.*

Cairn Terrier

height *small (10–12 ins; 25.5–30.5 cm)*
breed needs *Early and effective socialization with children is vital. Males can be feisty with other dogs if not socialized and trained.*

The Cairn Terrier offers liveliness, affability, and cheerfulness in a conveniently small package. Bred to hunt rats and foxes, the terrier instincts are ever-present, but combine well with a good responsiveness to training. The harsh, wiry coat comes in an array of different colors, ranging from cream to charcoal gray.

Czesky Terrier

height *medium (10–14 ins; 25.5–35.5 cm)*
breed needs *Early handling and grooming required, plus extra socialization. Czesky Terriers can be sharp and willful. For the experienced owner only.*
hereditary problems *Can suffer from Scottie cramp.*

With a long, low body, elongated head, and feathered coat, the Czesky Terrier is an unusual sight. In metallic blue-gray or tawny brown, the silky coat needs constant upkeep. Originally bred to burrow for ground vermin, this is a

right: *The outgoing Cairn Terrier.*

above: *Czesky Terriers need plenty of professional grooming.*

left: *A calm and gentle terrier— the Dandie Dinmont is sure to turn heads!*

typically feisty character that needs exercise and entertainment.

Dandie Dinmont Terrier/ Skye Terrier/Sealyham Terrier

height *medium (8–11 ins; 20.5–28 cm)*
breed needs *Unusual in character as well as appearance, this is a calm and gentle terrier! Responsive to affection and the comforts of a family home, this dog is suited to town or country.*
hereditary problems *Eye-testing necessary. Some back problems.*

A breed originating in the 1600s for badger hunting and ratting, the Dandie Dinmont is one of the most unusual of the terriers. Long and low, with a large, domed head, exaggerated by a ball of hair, the dog seems almost out of proportion.

Glen of Imaal Terrier

height *small (14 ins; 35.5 cm)*
breed needs *Positive early training and consistent, committed socialization with other dogs.*

A tough vermin hunter, this terrier was once used in dog fights in its native Ireland. Short and stocky, the breed retains fast reactions and a tendency to square up to other dogs if not socialized and trained. A rough-and-ready field companion.

above: *A rough-and-ready field companion—the Glen of Imaal Terrier.*

Jack Russell Terrier/ German Hunting Terrier

height *small (10–12 ins; 25.5–30.5 cm)*
breed needs *Simultaneously adored and hated, the Jack Russell can be snappy with people, especially children, and aggressive toward other dogs. They love digging and are rarely suited to living with small rodent pets. With good early socialization, however, they can be affectionate and fun-loving little dogs.*

The working man's terrier, the Jack Russell really is a Jack of all trades.

Small and powerfully muscled, these dogs vary enormously in size, shape, and color, although tri-color is probably the most common. A terrier through and through, this dog will hunt all day, has fast responses, and an infamously short fuse.

The German Hunting Terrier is remarkably similar, although black and tan, red, or brown and tan are the three coat colors. Strong-willed and determined, this dog needs work to do and training from an early age to become a practical and down-to-earth companion.

Kerry Blue Terrier

height *large (18–19 ins; 46–48 cm)*
breed needs *This dog loves water and outdoor pursuits. Males particularly need early socialization with other dogs.*

The distinctive color of this dog's coat gives its name to the breed. Originating in County Kerry, Ireland, this terrier has long been used as a tenacious rat and rabbit hunter and is an excellent guard dog. Born black, the coat lightens in color at around one year of age. The hair does not shed, making it appropriate for those with allergies to dog hair.

above: *Distinctive in shape, color, and personality, the Kerry Blue Terrier.*

left: *In characteristically alert pose, a Jack Russell Terrier.*

above: *A Norfolk Terrier, distinguishable from the Norwich by its "drop" ears.*

Norwich Terrier/ Norfolk Terrier

height *small (9.5–10.5 ins; 24.5–27 cm)*

breed needs *Remarkably unspoiled, these terriers know how to train human beings. Early handling, training, and socialization are essential, particularly with other small pets.*

The Norwich and Norfolk terriers are essentially very similar, apart from their ears, which are "drop" in the Norfolk and upright in the Norwich. Originally tenacious ratters, they are enthusiastic about exercise and love company.

left: *Staffordshire Bull Terrier.*

Soft-coated Wheaten Terrier

height *medium (18–19 ins; 46–48 cm)*

breed needs *Considering the relatively small numbers kept, the incidence of nervous Wheatens is currently high. Only buy from parents that are friendly and confident. The long, soft coat needs regular maintenance.*

hereditary problems *Hip and eye-testing necessary in parents.*

Bred in Ireland to act as a herder and vermin catcher, this dog has a coat the color of ripening wheat. Attractive and a good medium size, it is gaining in popularity.

Staffordshire Bull Terrier/American Staffordshire Bull Terrier

height *medium (14–16 ins; 35.5–40.5 cm)*

breed needs *Staffies and Am Staffs, their American cousins, can get along well with other dogs, but only if socialization starts immediately and is well maintained. Fighters are almost impossible to rehabilitate—their determination and the sheer force of massive jaws makes them potentially lethal adversaries.*

hereditary problems *Eye-testing necessary.*

above: *Gaining in popularity—the Soft-coated Wheaten Terrier.*

A medium-sized powerhouse, the Staffie is 38 pounds of pure muscle. With a short coat, broad head, and wide chest, this dog was originally bred in Britain for ratting and dog fights, but is an angel with people. Despite potential hostility toward other dogs and other animals, this dog is wonderfully gentle, loving, and affectionate toward the family.

Welsh Terrier/Irish Terrier

height *medium (Welsh 14–15.5 ins; 35.5–39 cm/Irish 18–19 ins; 46–48 cm)*

breed needs *Clean and smart dogs to have around the home, both these terriers can be trained to enjoy handling and have good social skills with people. Males, particularly, have a reputation for aggression with other dogs. Very early and extensive socialization and training are required to overcome this. Unsuitable with small pets.*

hereditary problems *Eye-testing in breeding stock required.*

Two terriers (not pictured) with an eye for mischief, the Welsh is an attractive black and tan, while the Irish is a stunning red. Both were bred as

and compact but muscular, neither of these breeds should be taken as lap dogs, for although they like home comforts, their ratting and digging instincts are always apparent.

Wire Fox Terrier/ Smooth Fox Terrier

height *medium (15 ins; 38 cm)*

breed needs *A tendency to be aggressive with other dogs, a "short fuse" with children and a willful disposition, this is a breed for the experienced owner only.*

hereditary problems *Eye-testing in breeding stock required. Some deafness in white dogs.*

The epitome of the true terrier—a compact, fiery breed with no fear and fast responses. The square stance and rigid outline of the breed give it an almost toy-like appearance, but this dog is not inclined to play.

left: *The Wire Fox Terrier is for experienced owners only.*

ratting dogs in the 1700s, and have retained much of their original working prowess.

West Highland White Terrier/Scottish Terrier

height *small (Westie 10–11 ins; 25.5–28 cm/Scottie 10–11 ins; 25.5–28 cm)*

breed needs *Early training, handling, and grooming are essential. These are large personalities in small frames. An aggressive or disgruntled Westie or Scottie can be impossible to live with.*

hereditary problems *Eye and skin problems prevalent. Legge Perthes disease.*

The pure white coat of the West Highland White Terrier is in stark contrast with the jet black of the Scottie, making them famous advertising companions. Both small

left: *The West Highland White Terrier is one half of a famous advertising duo for a brand of Scotch with its cousin, the Scottish Terrier, **right**.*

161

toy dogs

above: *Fluffy toys—the Bichon Frise and,* **below right***, the Bolognese.*

above: *The monkey-faced Affenpinscher.*

Affenpinscher

height *small (10–12 ins; 25.5–30.5 cm)*

breed needs *Substantial amounts of socialization and gentle handling required to prevent snappiness, particularly with children. Little coat maintenance required.*

With a little monkey face and rough coat, this dog looks and acts like his terrier ancestors—sparky and intelligent. Small but highly agile (it has the uncanny ability to climb) Affenpinschers are able to escape from even well-fenced enclosures.

Australian Silky Terrier

height *small (9 ins; 23 cm)*

breed needs *An affectionate and energetic dog, Australian Silky Terriers need extra socialization with other dogs when young, if only to ensure that they remain still and calm during greeting.*

A mixture of bloodlines from the Australian and Yorkshire terriers, the Australian Silky is a slightly larger version of the Yorkshire, with a lower maintenance coat. A neat, lively terrier, primarily bred as a companion.

Bichon Frise

height *small (9–11 ins; 23–28 cm)*

breed needs *Lively and curious, this small dog makes an ideal companion for those who are prepared to invest considerable amounts of time on coat maintenance.*

The Bichon's white, fluffy coat and jet-black eyes and nose are its trademarks. This is a compact dog, deceptively robust and energetic. The Bichon's tail curls over its back when alert.

Bolognese

height *small (10–12 ins; 25.5–30.5 cm)*

breed needs *A great deal of gentle early socialization required to increase confidence and prevent anxiety around strangers.*

Originally from Italy, the Bolognese is thought to have arisen as a breed in the Middle Ages. Similar in size and shape to the Bichon, its coat is rather more cotton-like, which presumably helps it to deal with a hot climate.

above: *The energetic and companionable Australian Silky Terrier.*

Chihuahua (smooth and longcoat)

height *small (6–9 ins; 15–23 cm)*

breed needs *A bright little dog, the Chihuahua can take well to training but needs early socialization to not behave defensively with strangers.*

hereditary problems *Slipping patella, heart problems.*

A miniature breed, the Chihuahua is delicate in every way. A true companion dog, this breed is happiest settled on your lap, although it can put on a ferocious guarding display if threatened. The heads of both short- and longcoated varieties are a distinctive "apple" shape—indeed, they are so domed that the fontenella (the point where the skull fuses after birth) is sometimes misshapen.

above: *The ultimate miniature dog, a smooth-coated Chihuahua.*

right: *The Cavalier King Charles Spaniel.*

Cavalier King Charles Spaniel/ King Charles Spaniel

height *medium*
(Cavalier 12–13 ins; 30.5–33 cm/ King Charles 10–11 ins; 25.5–28 cm)

breed needs *A happy, cheerful, and friendly dog, the Cavalier is one of the most reliable and flexible of family pets—content to rest on the sofa with you, or trek hills and fields instead.*

hereditary problems *Sadly, this breed has considerable heart problems and hip dysplasia. Heart testing vital. Eye testing for breeding stock recommended.*

The Cavalier has become increasingly popular in recent years—and deservedly so. A medium-sized, well-balanced dog, with a long, silky coat, well-rounded head, and expressive eyes. Colors vary from solid "ruby," to tri-color, black and tan, and Blenheim (white and tan). The King Charles is often confused with the Cavalier, but has a compressed muzzle and turned-up nose.

Chinese Crested Dog

height *small (9–13 ins; 23–33 cm)*
breed needs *Hairless dogs always require protection from the cold and can get sunburned in extreme conditions. The powder-puffs need considerable attention to the coat.*

One of the most distinctive breeds in the world, the Chinese Crested is noted for the total absence of hair on all parts of its body apart from its head, feet, and tip of the tail. Because such nakedness is a genetic peculiarity, litters always include normally coated puppies, called "powder-puffs." These dogs have long, flowing hair all over.

English Toy Terrier

height *small (10–12 ins; 25.5–33 cm)*
breed needs *Early socialization to avoid anxiety around other dogs and noises of all kinds.*

Lithe, sleek, and always a distinctive black and tan coloration, the English Toy Terrier may be dainty, but it's fast!

Originally bred as a miniature version of the Manchester Terrier, it has a ratting ancestry.

Griffon Bruxellois

height *small (7–8 ins; 17.5–20.5 cm)*
breed needs *Exercise and mental stimulation are important for this breed. Socialization, especially with children, needs to be ongoing.*
hereditary problems *Patella defects.*

Rough-coated and monkey-faced, this feisty companion dog has its roots in terrier ancestry, making it lively and outgoing. The smooth-coated version, called Petit Brabancon, is regarded as a different breed in its native Belgium, and has a pug-like face.

top: *The rough-coated and exotically named Griffon Bruxellois.*

left: *Highly distinctive, the Chinese Crested needs protection from both the sun and cold.*

far left: *An English Toy Terrier.*

Maltese

height *small (8–10 ins; 20.5–25.5 cm)*

breed needs *As the coat never sheds, good grooming is essential.*

hereditary problems *Patella luxation.*

The long, white, flowing coat of the Maltese (not pictured) is highly distinctive. This dog is primarily a companion, and enjoys exercise as well as affection.

Miniature Pinscher

height *small (10–12 ins; 25.5–30.5 cm)*

breed needs *A good-sized dog to keep where space is limited, mental stimulation and early socialization are important to prevent snappiness or excessive barking.*

hereditary problems *Slipping patella.*

A small dog with a big personality, the Miniature Pinscher may look like a tiny Doberman, but was, in fact, bred for ratting along quite different lines. Neat and lively, this little dog's movement is perhaps its most remarkable feature—picking up the front feet in a hackney fashion when at a trot.

Italian Greyhound

height *medium (13–15 ins; 33–38 cm)*

breed needs *Early, gentle handling is important. They are generally friendly and outgoing, but nothing looks more sad than an anxious, shivering Italian Greyhound. Very little coat care required— they rarely shed.*

An ancient breed in heritage, this sleek, fast-moving breed is delicate, but still enjoys exercise as much as home comforts. Medium in size, the Italian Greyhound has a high-stepping, almost hackney action when trotting.

Lowchen

height *medium (10–13 ins; 25.5–33 cm)*

breed needs *Early and effective socialization with other dogs is a must for this breed. The coat requires structured clipping for the show ring.*

hereditary problems *Slipping patella.*

Usually clipped over the rear end, with the front end forming a mane of hair, it's no wonder that the Lowchen is sometimes called the "Little Lion Dog." Robust in body and spirit, this medium-sized dog originated in France in the 1600s, primarily for use as a companion.

above: *The Italian Greyhound has an ancient heritage.*

top left: *The "Little Lion Dog," or Lowchen, requires substantial early socialization with other dogs.*

above: *The Miniature Pinscher—a strong personality in a miniature frame.*

above: *This picture beautifully displays the Papillon's butterfly ears.*

Long, flowing hair, a compressed face, and large, round eyes give this dog an Oriental, even haughty expression.

Pomeranian

height *small (8.5–11 ins; 22–28 cm)*
breed needs *Poms are intelligent and quick to learn. Many excel at obedience training and even mini-agility tests. May be prone to barking if not prevented early on.*
hereditary problems *Patella defects.*

A true spitz in miniature, the Pomeranian possesses all the behavioral and physical characteristics of many larger spitz breeds in a diminutive form. A huge ruff of hair around the

Papillon

height *small (8–11 ins; 20.5–28 cm)*
breed needs *Highly trainable, the Papillon thrives on attention and mental stimulation.*
hereditary problems *Slipping patella and heart problems.*

Often known as the "butterfly" dog, the Papillon's name no doubt comes from its heavily feathered ears, which form "butterfly wings" when the dog is alert. Compact, with a spitz-type tail and delicate features, these beautiful dogs are also intelligent and respond well to training.

Pekingese

height *small (6–9 ins; 15–23 cm)*
breed needs *Effective socialization with people, children, and other dogs is important. The long coat requires regular maintenance.*
hereditary problems *Occasional back problems. Protruding eyes may be prone to injury.*

The sacred dog of the Chinese Royal Courts, the Pekingese was reputed to live in the flowing sleeves of dignitaries. Heavy for its size, and with bowed legs, Pekes are not known for their activity, but are nonetheless bright and courageous.

below: *This black Pekingese shows off the breed's large round eyes to perfection.*

Yorkshire Terrier

height *small (9 ins; 23 cm)*

breed needs *Do not be fooled by the Yorkie's size—this dog has a big personality and is a true terrier in nature. A lack of early socialization, combined with overprotective owners, can result in aggression to owners, people, and other dogs. However, Yorkies are bright sparks, and respond well to early motivational training.*

hereditary problems *Dentition problems. Some respiratory defects. Slipping patella.*

In full show condition, a Yorkie's hair is a full-length skirt, trailing on the floor. A magnificent steel and tan, it is no wonder that these little dogs are so popular, even if most owners opt for a practical all-over trim. Diminutive in size and weighing only 5 pounds in some cases, Yorkies may seem small and fragile, but they are giants in behavior and attitude to life.

neck and a profusely coated tail, held over the back when alert, make this breed look larger-than-life.

Pug

height *small (10–11 ins; 25.5–28 cm)*

breed needs *Although strong-willed, Pugs are usually friendly with people and other animals. Owners soon get used to their somewhat noisy breathing—and learn to sleep through their snoring.*

above: *Bright and cheerful—two wonderful Pomeranians.*

hereditary problems *Occasional hip dysplasia. Protruding eyes may be prone to injury. Occasional respiratory problems.*

The Pug's flat face is one of the most well-known in the canine world. Square in body shape and compact, the wrinkled head and large round eyes emphasize its inquisitive and pugnacious personality.

above: *Its steely gray and tan coloring contribute to the Yorkie's enduring popularity as a pet and show dog.*

above: *The inquisitive and wrinkled brow, flat face, and tightly curled tail are the instantly recognizable trademarks of the Pug.*

utility dogs
those bred for "specialized" tasks

above: *At attention—the Boston Terrier.*

Boston Terrier

height *medium (15–17 ins; 38–43 cm)*

breed needs *An outgoing, cheerful dog, Boston Terriers have lost most of their ratting ancestry and prefer the company of people. Can be noisy if untrained or unsocialized.*

hereditary problems *Eye defects. Slipping patella.*

A neat, medium-sized dog, the Boston Terrier has clean lines, with character radiating from every pore. It has a large head with a flattened nose, although this is not exaggerated as in some similar breeds. Upright, triangular ears give the appearance of alertness. They have a short, low maintenance coat.

Bulldog

height *medium (12–14 ins; 30.5–35.5 cm)*

breed needs *Usually docile and friendly, the Bulldog's sometimes noisy breathing and excessive snoring may take some getting used to. Males need careful and ongoing socialization with other dogs.*

hereditary problems *Respiratory problems. Natural birth impossible for many.*

The Bulldog is universally known for its stocky, square shape, and wide,

flattened nose. Originally bred for bull-baiting, this dog was a great deal taller and less exaggerated than those seen today, which are kept solely as companions.

Chow Chow

height *large (18–22 ins; 46–56 cm)*

breed needs *Chows can be stubborn, aloof, and even belligerent. With very early, ongoing, and committed socialization, they can be humorous, affectionate clowns with a unique "I own the world" attitude to life.*

hereditary problems *Entropion.*

An ancient Chinese breed, the Chow was originally prized as an edible delicacy, with a fur coat to offer as a

above: *A rough-coated Chow Chow.*

bonus! Those that avoided the dinner table were also regarded as good guard dogs. The Chow comes in two versions—rough and smooth. The better-known rough has a huge, fluffy

below: *The modern Bulldog is an exaggerated version of its forebears.*

left: *Walt Disney almost turned the Dalmatian into an institution, but its size and energy can make it unsuitable for the inexperienced owner.*

French Bulldog

height *small (12 ins; 30.5 cm)*

breed needs *Characteristic snuffling breathing and potential snoring. Busy and curious by nature.*

hereditary problems *Potential back problems.*

Short-legged and stocky, the French Bulldog was originally a ratter, but is now a companion. A flattened face and short pug-like nose with upright ears give a characteristic expression— either loved or hated. The short, smooth coat can be in many color variations—pied, white, and black are the most common.

above: *The German Spitz. This is the smallest of the three types.*

German Spitz

height *Giant (16 ins; 40.5 cm),
Standard (14 ins; 35.5 cm),
Toy (9–11 ins; 23–28 cm)*

breed needs *All three varieties are bright and self-occupied. Training and early socialization are essential. Can be noisy in the house and outside.*

hereditary problems *Slipping patella.*

There are three sizes of German Spitz: Giant (gross), Standard (mittel), and Toy (klein). All three are a classic spitz shape, with profuse coats that stand off from the body for increased insulation, small upright ears, and a curled tail.

coat that extends over neck and head to give an overall "teddy bear" appearance. Both versions have a black tongue.

Dalmatian

height *large (20–24 ins; 51–61 cm)*

breed needs *Those who purchase a Dalmatian on the basis of a Disney movie or as a fashion accessory will not cope for long. Dalmatians are highly trainable, but need extra socialization when young (males can be aggressive with other dogs if not) and sensitive, careful training over a long period. Deafness is prevalent in the breed, which can make training this large, boisterous dog even more of a challenge.*

hereditary problems *Deafness.*

Bred to trot for miles behind the carriages of the rich and well-to-do, and sometimes as a hunter, the Dalmatian or "carriage dog" has boundless energy and a mind of its own. Unique in appearance, the smooth, white coat of this large, elegant breed is spotted all over in black or liver, making it instantly recognizable.

right: *A French Bulldog with the characteristic pug-like nose.*

Japanese Akita

height *large (24–28 ins; 61–71 cm)*
breed needs *Considerable motivational training and socialization with other dogs required. Males particularly can be aggressive toward other dogs.*
hereditary problems *Eye problems.*

Originally bred in Japan for dog fighting, then kept as a large game-hunter, this is a strong, powerful breed. Upright ears and a square stance give the dog an aloof and superior presence. The tail curls over the back when the Akita is alert.

Japanese Shiba Inu

height *medium (14–16 ins; 35.5–40.5 cm)*
breed needs *Early recall training and good socialization with other dogs essential. The Shiba does not bark—it shrieks when alarmed or frustrated.*
hereditary problems *Patella and hock problems.*

above: *The Leonberger, a gentle giant.*

above left: *The Japanese Akita.*

This fox-like dog from Japan has an ancient history. Originally bred as a hunter of small mammals and birds, it is becoming increasingly popular as a companion in other countries. Curious and cat-like in behavior, this is a medium-sized breed with a plush coat and a superior expression.

Japanese Spitz

height *medium (12–14 ins; 30.5–35.5 cm)*
breed needs *Can be noisy, and barks for the sake of hearing its own voice if not trained to behave otherwise.*
hereditary problems *Patella luxation.*

Probably a scaled down version of the Samoyed, this pure white spitz from Japan has all its larger cousin's characteristics, without the size. Large, dark eyes, set in a sea of white luxurious coat makes this a striking dog.

Leonberger

height *large (26–31.5 ins; 66–79.5 cm)*
breed needs *Early socialization to ensure calm, quiet confidence. As with all giant breeds, exercise and diet should be carefully monitored during growth.*
hereditary problems *Eye, hip, and elbow testing recommended.*

A massive, distinguished breed, the Leonberger is tall and heavy, but still remarkably agile. A gentle expression, with brown eyes and a dark mask, make this an approachable gentle giant.

left: *The strikingly beautiful Japanese Spitz.*

Lhasa Apso/Shih Tzu

height *small (10–11 ins; 25.5–28 cm)*
breed needs *The Shih Tzu tends to be more affable and playful than the Lhasa, which can be aloof and rather superior.*
hereditary problems *Some eye defects.*

While similar in looks, the Lhasa and the Shih Tzu have quite different origins. The Lhasa originated in Tibet, from ancient times, and was used as an advance warning system by the monks of Tibet, as it would bark at the slightest sound. The Shih Tzu comes from China, where it was bred as a companion for the emperor. Both breeds have long, flowing hair that almost completely covers the length of the dog.

Poodle—Toy/Miniature/Standard

height *large (Standard over 15 ins; 38 cm), medium (Miniature 11–15 ins; 28–38 cm), and small (Toy under 11 ins; 28 cm)*
breed needs *Playful and curious, even into old age, the Poodle is an intelligent fast learner. These*

dogs can excel at obedience, agility, and other dog "sports," but can become "self-employed" if not given a job to do.
hereditary problems *Hip dysplasia. Eye testing recommended. Skin problems.*

Poodles of all sizes are strong and athletic. Built as water dogs, to retrieve game and birds, the characteristic "clip" was used to protect the joints from cold. Different sizes arose from the breed's popularity as a companion. The coat is non-shedding and tightly curled, and needs considerable maintenance, even if kept in a pet clip.

above: *The high-maintenance Poodle with characteristic "show clip."*

left: *Two inquisitive Shih Tzu and,* **above,** *their Oriental cousin, the Lhasa Apso.*

Schipperke

height *small (9–13 ins; 23–33 cm)*

breed needs *Can be short-tempered with both children and other dogs. Early and careful socialization with other household pets required.*

A neat, confident little dog, the Schipperke was bred to guard Dutch and Belgian barges, taking up little room and requiring little maintenance. This all-purpose dog also kept the boats clear of vermin, and retains its terrier-type instincts encased in a spitz-like body.

Schnauzer (Miniature), Schnauzer (Standard)

height *medium (Standard, under 19 ins; 48 cm), and small (Miniature, under 14 ins; 35.5 cm)*

breed needs *Schnauzers of all sizes are intelligent, with a real work ethic. They can excel at obedience and mini-agility, if trained carefully with motivational methods.*

Officially, the different sizes of Schnauzer reside in different Kennel Club groups—the Miniature and Standard sizes in the Utility Group, and the Giant in the Working Group. Bred in Germany in the Middle Ages, the compact, sturdy outline of the breed has changed little over the years. A combination of terrier, spitz, and guarding blood must be present. Their coats are harsh, in gray ("salt and pepper") or black, while their heads are distinguished by a huge mustache of hair and bushy eyebrows.

above: *The Schipperke was originally bred to act as a guard onboard canal barges.*

below: *A handsome Miniature Schnauzer shows off its bristling "salt and pepper" mustache.*

Shar Pei

height *large (18–20 ins; 46–51 cm)*

breed needs *Huge amounts of socialization required for these dogs, with other dogs in particular. Considerable coat and skin care required.*

hereditary problems *Entropion. Skin problems.*

A powerfully built dog in a skin two sizes too big! Bred in China for fighting other dogs, legend has it that the Shar Pei can turn around in its own skin to face its adversary! Harsh hair and a massive head confirm this dog's original role.

Tibetan Spaniel

height *small (10 ins; 25.5 cm)*

breed needs *Bright little dogs, with clean habits, Tibetan Spaniels can be strong-willed, but open to sensitive and consistent learning.*

hereditary problems *Eye defects.*

An ancient breed, the Tibetan Spaniel was reputed to turn the monks' prayer wheels in the monasteries of its homeland. A small dog in build only, it has no resemblance to the Spaniels, but is distinctly Oriental in appearance.

above: *A trio of Tibetan Spaniels.*

below: *A Tibetan Terrier showing its long, luxuriant coat.*

Tibetan Terrier

height *medium (14–16 ins; 35.5–40.5 cm)*

breed needs *This dog's ability to guard the home is based on a wariness of strangers—often highly inappropriate in a domestic situation. Tibetan Terriers can be nervous if not socialized early, with as many different people as possible.*

hereditary problems *Hip dysplasia. Eye defects.*

Certainly this long-coated, dignified breed originated from Tibet—but not as a terrier. In outline this dog is stocky and compact in a medium-sized frame. Its head and eyes are completely covered by long, flowing hair. Bred as a companion dog.

left: *The powerful Shar Pei with classic wrinkling.*

working dogs

including **spitz-types** and **pastoral dogs**, such as **sheepdogs** and **flock-guarders**

Australian Cattle Dog/ Kelpie/Corgi/Cardigan/ Pembroke/Lancashire Heeler

height *large (Australian Cattle Dog/Kelpie 17–20 ins; 43–51 cm), small (Lancashire Heeler 10–12 ins; 25.5–30.5 cm/ Cardigan Corgi 10.5–12.5 ins; 27–32 cm/ Pembroke Corgi 10–12 ins; 25.5–30.5 cm)*

breed needs *All heelers, not surprisingly, are prone to heeling! This means that children, other dogs, and even adults can be victims of ankle nips without training and early socialization.*

hereditary problems *Eye defects.*

The Australian Cattle Dog is a true heeler, bred to nip at the ankles of cattle to drive them along. A substantial dog, compact and strong without any exaggeration, with a powerful, square muzzle. Other heelers bred for similar work include the Kelpie, a native of Australia, the smaller Lancashire Heeler, and the Corgi from Britain.

Belgian Shepherd/ Dutch Shepherd

height *large (22–26 ins; 56–66 cm)*

breed needs *All the Belgian Shepherd varieties are highly trainable, but require great socialization and habituation to avoid nervousness or overprotective behavior.*

hereditary problems *Eye defects.*

Controversy reigns over the Belgian Shepherd—with some kennel clubs insisting it is one breed encapsulating four varieties, and others classifying them as four separate breeds. All the versions were bred in Belgium for livestock herding. They are lithe and athletic, with substantial muscle on a slender frame. Their heads are narrow, ears large and upright. The four varieties are:

Groenendael: Black and long-coated, with a distinct "wolf" appearance created by the large ruff of hair around the neck.

Tervueren: Long-coated in shades of gray, fawn, and red, usually with darker markings on muzzle and back.

Malinois: A short coat in red, fawn, or gray, with a dark mask.

Laekenois: Dense, fawn-colored, semi-curled coat all over, including the head and ears.

Bernese Mountain Dog/ Great Swiss Mountain Dog/ Entelbuch Mountain Dog

height *large (Bernese/Great Swiss Mountain Dog 23–27.5 ins; 58.5–70 cm; Entelbuch Mountain Dog 23.5–28.5 ins; 60–72 cm)*

breed needs *The Great Swiss Mountain Dog and Entelbuch Mountain Dog are rarely seen outside of their native lands. The Bernese is a happy-go-lucky character, needing early training if not to overwhelm people with over-affectionate greetings.*

hereditary problems *Hip dysplasia and elbow problems.*

All three of these breeds originate from Switzerland and were bred primarily for drafting. Large and heavy-boned, they are tri-colored, with expressive, gentle features and wide-set ears. The Bernese has a silky, long coat.

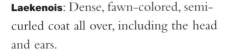

top right: *A Cardigan Corgi.*
left: *A Bernese Mountain Dog.*

left: *The ever popular Bearded Collie and,* **right,** *a pair of tri-colored Boxers.*

Border Collie/Bearded Collie

height *large*

(Border Collie 18–21 ins; 46–53.5 cm/ Bearded Collie 20–22 ins; 51–56 cm)

breed needs *Quick to learn, Collies tend to fit into patterns of behavior that can be constructive in the field or destructive in the home. Their desire to fix an eye on a moving object, stalk it, and chase it is inherent, and makes joggers, other animals, and even children prone to being herded if the drive is frustrated. Responsive to training and repetition of tasks, the Collie is hard-working and determined. Needs consistent, long-term training, and substantial mental and physical stimulation. The most common breed for behavior problems, due to popularity and a lack of understanding about the breed's need to work.*

hereditary problems *Hip and eye testing advised. Some deafness.*

Perhaps the most popular working dog in the United Kingdom, the Border Collie is hard working and quick to learn. A substantial dog, its appearance varies greatly, as many are still bred from working stock, not show specimens. Nearly always long-coated, classically black and white or tri-color, and built for speed, it is athletic and well-muscled. The Beardie is similar in size and shape, but has a long, straight coat and a playful personality.

Bouvier Des Flandres/Briard

height *Bouvier large (23–27 ins; 58.5–68.5 cm), Briard large (23–27 ins; 58.5–68.5 cm)*

breed needs *Very early effective socialization required for both these breeds. Can be strong-willed and aggressive to other dogs if not raised and trained carefully.*

hereditary problems *Hip dysplasia. Eye testing for Briards.*

Square and powerful, the Bouvier was developed as a cattle drover in Belgium in the 1600s. Heavily bearded, with a thick, wavy coat of harsh hair, it is stoic and enduring.

The Briard has long, flowing hair, an expressive face, and a strong, straight back. Bred to herd and guard livestock, it is now a popular French pet.

Boxer

height *large (21–25 ins; 53.5–63.5 cm)*

breed needs *The "clown with a heart" aptly describes most Boxers. Playful and active, even into their mature years, Boxers need early training, even if only to protect visitors from over-exuberant greetings! Males need above-average amounts of socialization with other dogs.*

hereditary problems *Hip dysplasia. Serious heart problems—breeding stock must be tested.*

A well-muscled, lean dog, with a broad chest and square outline, the Boxer's face is its trademark—its flattened nose and powerful jaw certainly live up to its name! Bred in Germany for bull-baiting and guarding, these dogs were among those tenacious enough to cling onto the bull's nose, yet friendly enough to live as a house dog.

left: *The heavily bearded Bouvier Des Flandres from Belgium.*

left: *A Bullmastiff.*

Training can be successful using motivational and patient methods.

hereditary problems *Hip dysplasia. Some potential eye problems.*

Bred to guard property in Britain in the 1800s, the Bullmastiff is powerfully built, muscular, and solid. A slightly flattened muzzle and wrinkled head gives an appealing expression. Other mastiffs in the same family are even heavier, and more excessively wrinkled than the Bullmastiff.

Bullmastiff/Mastiff/ Neopolitan Mastiff/ Brazilian Mastiff

height *large (25–27 ins; 63.5–68.5 cm)*
breed needs *Ideally affable and calm, Bullmastiffs need early training and socialization if they are to reach full potential as family members.*

Doberman

height *large (25.5–27 ins; 65–68.5 cm)*
breed needs *Early socialization is vital for this intelligent, hard-working breed. They can be clownish and playful if bred and raised in the right manner, nervous and aggressive if not.*
hereditary problems *Eye testing for parents and puppies recommended.*

Lean and muscular, the Doberman is elegant and sleek. Always black and tan, with a smooth coat, this dog was bred in Germany to guard the home. Cropped ears and a docked tail used to be the order of the day. Fortunately, such practices are becoming less and less common.

German Shepherd Dog

height *large (22–26 ins; 56–66 cm)*
breed needs *The most perfect family pet or the worst behavioral nightmare, the German Shepherd Dog represents one of the most ambivalent of breeds. Temperament and behavior have been adversely affected by unscrupulous breeding for profit and to alter the dog's role from a herder to a guarding breed. Buy from a carefully selected breeder and socialize from birth, especially with other dogs. Eminently trainable in the right hands, aggressive and fearful if not.*
hereditary problems *Hip dysplasia. Males need to be tested for hemophilia before breeding.*

left: *The German Shepherd, or Alsatian, has its origins in herding—not guarding.*

Possibly the best known and loved of all the working breeds, the German Shepherd Dog, or Alsatian, is easily recognized. Usually black and tan with a short coat, it can be any color from white to jet black, or long-coated. A long, noble head, with alert expression and large, upright ears, on a long, often sloping body, with hind angulation built for speed. Originally developed as a livestock herder, the herding instinct is still strong in many individuals, and is often misinterpreted as protection.

Giant Schnauzer

height *large*
(23.5–27.5 ins; 60–70 cm)
breed needs *Can be playful and trainable. Males, particularly, can be aggressive toward other dogs, so early and consistent socialization is necessary.*

The giant version of the smaller Miniature and Standard cousins, the Giant Schnauzer is a stocky, strong breed, with athletic ability. Tenacity and stamina have led this breed to be

right: *The stocky profile of a Giant Schnauzer contrasts with the sleek look of a Doberman,* **opposite page**.

used as a police dog—contrasting with its original role as a livestock herder in Germany.

Great Dane

height *large (28–30 ins; 71–76 cm)*
breed needs *Early socialization with other dogs is essential. Basic obedience training, using motivational methods, is also wise with a dog of this size.*
hereditary problems *Some eye defects.*

The sheer size of the Great Dane makes it a famous breed. Long and elegant, this dog is well-balanced and capable of a good turn of speed, despite its height. Bred to hunt wild boar, there is some dispute as to its origins—Germany seems more likely than Denmark.

Hungarian Kuvasz

height *large (26–29.5 ins; 66–75 cm)*
breed needs *Considerable amounts of early socialization required. Experienced owners are best for this independent breed.*

Bred to rest among sheep, to protect them from wolves and other predators, the Kuvasz is a gentle giant unless roused to duty. Always pale in color, to blend with the flock, it is a large and powerful breed, with a good turn of speed, if needed.

left: *The giant Great Dane.*

right: *The Hungarian Kuvasz is perfectly camouflaged to hide among sheep.*

Komondor

height *large (26.5–35.5 ins; 67–90 cm)*
breed needs *The "dreadlock" coat needs considerable time and attention to prevent matting. Early socialization also required.*
hereditary problems *Hip testing advised.*

The amazing, oily, corded coat of this Hungarian breed (not pictured) acts as protection against the cold and as armor against predators. This is a flock-guarding breed, designed to blend in with sheep in the field and wander amenably among them. Large and powerful, it can transform from lamb to lion temperament when necessary.

left: *Bred to resist the icy Canadian waters, the Newfoundland is still working in water rescue.*

A huge tug-boat of a dog, the Newfoundland was bred to brave the icy waters off Canada, and to pull both fishing nets and boats in to shore. Jet black or the richest brown, their coats are full and water-resistant, while their feet are webbed to assist swimming. Newfies are still used for water rescue work today.

Old English Sheepdog

height *large (22–24 ins; 56–61 cm)*
breed needs *Big and bouncy, these dogs need early and substantial amounts of training.*
hereditary problems *Hip dysplasia and eye problems.*

Large and powerful, the Old English Sheepdog, or Bobtail, as it is sometimes called, was originally a sheep herder. A huge, fluffy coat is now the breed's best-known feature, often clipped to make care of pet dogs easier.

Mudi

height *large (14–20 ins; 35.5–51 cm)*
breed needs *Despite its flexibility and working skills, the Mudi is not commonplace, even in Hungary. Early socialization and training are required to get the best out of this natural dog.*

A truly rare breed, the Mudi (not pictured) is seldom seen outside its native Hungary, where it is used as a flock guarder and herder. An alert-looking breed, with a sharp head and round eyes, it is a well-balanced working dog. The dense and wavy coat can be any color.

Newfoundland

height *large (26–28 ins; 66–71 cm)*
breed needs *Friendly and outgoing, most Newfies need basic training to control their natural exuberance as youngsters. They love swimming and cannot resist water.*
hereditary problems *Hip dysplasia. Heart-testing recommended.*

right: *Famous for its fluffy coat, the Old English Sheepdog.*

right: *The unusual looking Pumi, a shepherd from Hungary, is little known compared to the magnificent Pyrenean Mountain Dog,* **below**.

Pumi

height *large (13–19 ins; 33–48 cm)*

breed needs *A true working dog, the Pumi is sparky and full of stamina, and can be vociferous.*

This little-known breed from Hungary was used to herd cattle and sheep. Its black coat is rugged and semi-curled, which prevents matting. Its head is almost triangular, with unique ears— curled over at the tips and covered with feathering.

and bitches is more diverse than in many other breeds—females are often easier to train and more biddable than males, who can be rather strong-willed and difficult with other dogs.

hereditary problems *Eye defects. Dermoid sinus.*

Strong, compact, and powerful, the Rottweiler combines sheer muscle power with endurance. A square dog, with a broad chest and massive head. Its black and tan markings emphasize an intelligent expression. Originally bred as a cattle herder and guard dog.

Pyrenean Mountain Dog/Great Pyrenees

height *large (26–32 ins; 66–81 cm)*

breed needs *A dog for those with sufficient space at home! Pyreneans require gentle training and ample grooming.*

A true flock guarder, Pyreneans were originally kept to protect sheep from marauding wolves. This required the gentleness of a lamb, plus the tenacity of the wolf itself. The sheer size of the Pyrenean, plus its magnificent pale coat, make it an elegant dog, usually gentle with people.

Rottweiler

height *(23–27 ins; 58.5–68.5 cm)*

breed needs *Despite its flexibility and training ease, the Rottweiler has received much bad press. Aggression problems have largely been addressed by responsible breeders. The behavior of dogs*

right: *The powerhouse Rottweiler.*

above: *The spitz-shaped Samoyed.*

Samoyed

height *large (18–22 ins; 46–56 cm)*
breed needs *Large and boisterous, Samoyeds need early training to ensure familiarity with people and acceptance of being groomed. They are a breed that like the sound of their own voice—necessitating effective training or tolerant neighbors!*

left: *The Rough Collie, made famous by Hollywood.*

Rough Collie/ Smooth Collie/ Shetland Sheepdog

height *large (18–21 ins; 46–53.5 cm), Shetland Sheepdog medium (14–15 ins; 35.5–38 cm)*
breed needs *The Rough Collie has a profuse coat, which needs constant maintenance and grooming. The Smooth Collie is much more "wash and wear," but is perhaps not so glamorous.*
hereditary problems *Eye problems. Hip dysplasia in Shetland.*

Although used as a sheep herder in the 1800s, this British-bred dog did not achieve true popularity as a pet until the release of the *Lassie* movies—which may have given the impression that they would understand English! The Shetland Sheepdog is a miniature version of the Rough Collie. It can be highly sound-sensitive and needs careful early habituation to noises of all kinds.

right: *The Alaskan Malamute is heavier than its cousin the Siberian Husky,* **opposite top.**

A true sled dog, with basic drives, the Siberian Husky is smaller and lighter than its heavier cousin the Malamute. Both are affectionate and loyal to their owners, although they can be aloof with strangers. Well-balanced and wolf-like in shape, these dogs are still used for their original task of sled-pulling, both in their native lands of Siberia and in the United States, and in racing competitions elsewhere. One eye brown, the other blue or two blue eyes are common.

A classic spitz-shape, with a profuse coat that stands off from the body, the Samoyed is always pure white in color, as it was used to guard and sometimes hunt reindeer in the snowy areas of Russia.

Siberian Husky/ Alaskan Malamute

height *large*

(Siberian Husky 20–23.5 ins; 51–60 cm, Malamute 23–28 ins; 58.5–71 cm)

breed needs *Both these breeds work well for those who understand their need to fit into the family as part of a "pack" and give them something to do. Extra socialization with other dogs required as pups to avoid aggression problems. Can be highly destructive if left alone.*

hereditary problems *Eye testing for breeding stock recommended.*

right: *The St. Bernard is regarded as the Good Samaritan of the utility dog world.*

St. Bernard

height *large (24–28 ins; 61–71 cm)*

breed needs *Sadly, this is not a long-lived breed, because of hereditary defects. Early socialization is essential. St. Bernards are known for their gentle nature, but a few aggressive specimens have blotted an otherwise unsullied history.*

hereditary problems *Hip dysplasia. Heart problems.*

Legendary for rescuing lost travelers in the snow-covered mountains of Switzerland, St. Bernards have been kept by monks at the Bernardine Hospice in the Alps since the 1660s, primarily as draft dogs. A massive breed, huge in bone and head, they are long-coated or smooth.

breeding

Many owners dream of having puppies from their bitch. Of course, this can be a wonderful experience—allowing children to appreciate the processes involved in reproduction, as well as providing puppies to continue your favorite dog's line.

However, some home truths need to be realized first. Rearing puppies is hard work and—contrary to uneducated belief—is rarely profitable. You may have sleepless nights, the cleaning up seems endless, the mother needs constant care, and all puppies need handling, socialization, veterinary attention, and good new homes once they are ready to leave Mom. There are already far too many unwanted dogs in the world, so do think carefully before breeding any more.

selecting a mate

Most pedigree dogs are mated to others of the same breed. The choice of mate is dependent on whether or not you show or work your dog, and would hope to keep a pup for showing or working, too. Most matings are intended to produce offspring that take the best from both dog and bitch, so the male's attributes should complement the bitch's.

Occasionally, matings between two different breeds are carried out deliberately to combine the best characteristics of each breed in one dog. The "Labradoodle" is a first cross between the Labrador and the Standard Poodle, designed to produce a dog that has the intelligence of both breeds with the added advantage of minimum hair loss—since Poodles do not shed hair.

when to mate

Bleeding usually indicates the onset of the bitch's season. This lasts between four days and two weeks. It is only after the bleeding finishes that the bitch is fertile. This stage lasts between

above: *A Bull Terrier bitch expecting puppies. Only in the latter stages of pregnancy can physical changes be seen.*

five and twelve days. Mating is usually most successful if the bitch is mated at the beginning of this time, then again two days later.

below: *Contented four-day-old puppies suckle from their mother. Eyes and ears are not yet open.*

---

some useful tips

It is not true that a bitch needs to have a litter, and it won't cure a behavioral problem.

Your bitch must have a perfect temperament. Her puppies could well learn these same traits, or they may be passed on genetically.

A bitch should never be bred in her first season. Kennel clubs will not accept registrations for puppies born to bitches over eight years old.

Make sure your puppies are really wanted. Secure homes for them before you even mate your bitch.

You may wish to register your puppies with the kennel club. This can only be done if your bitch is purebred and she is already registered.

Many breeds now have hereditary problems, and testing programs are available to prevent these from being passed on inadvertently. If your bitch is of a breed that requires such testing, ensure that both she and the stud dog have been examined prior to mating.

It is usually unwise to use a male pet dog as the stud. Giving him a taste of what he has been missing is likely to create frustration and possibly even aggression toward other male dogs.

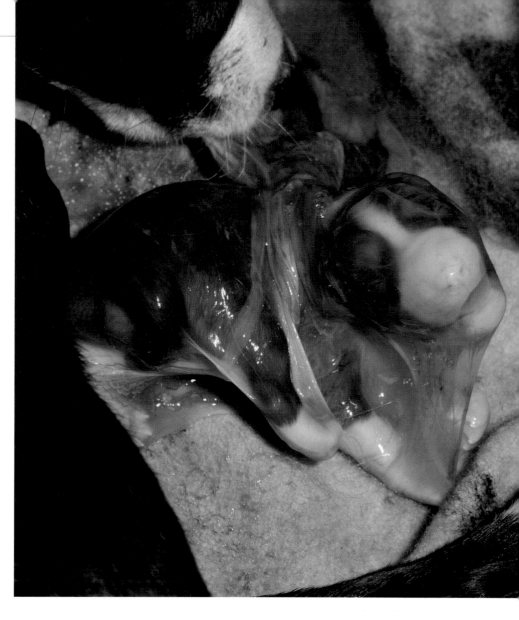

right: *A Border Collie bitch cleans her third puppy to remove the fetal membrane.*

Most stud dog owners require that the bitch be brought to them. If she is not ready, you may have to be patient and bring her back again until she decides the time is right.

pregnancy

The average length of a bitch's pregnancy is 63 days. It may be difficult to tell whether the bitch is in whelp until the fifth week, although scanning is now available at larger veterinary practices. Even at this stage a healthy bitch shows few physical changes. Her teats may swell and darken, and she may need to urinate more often, but her requirements for food and exercise remain the same.

Only in the final few weeks of pregnancy do most bitches require a little extra food—preferably with high quality protein.

the birth

Although it is unusual for bitches to whelp more than a day or two either side of the 63 days, it is not unheard of—so be prepared.

Whelping boxes are usually made of wood or plastic. The sides are usually about 18 inches (46 cm) in height on three sides, with the fourth left open, with just a low ridge to keep out drafts. Inside the box a narrow guardrail is fixed about 4 inches (10 cm) above the base. This is to prevent the puppies from accidentally being pushed against the sides of the box by their mother.

The whelping box needs to be placed in a fairly calm spot in the house, so you will be able to keep an eye on the new family without constant disturbance.

left: *Labor is physically tiring for any bitch, but previous good health and care assists her at this time.*

Some breeders use an overhead infrared lamp to keep the puppies warm. While this may be needed if temperatures are extremely low, or if the pups are whelped outdoors in a kennel, inside a warm room this should not be necessary.

About 12 hours before a bitch is due to whelp her temperature drops to below 100°F (38°C), and this is a sure sign. Some behavioral changes also suggest that birth is imminent—your dog is likely to refuse food, and may seem restless. Once the waters have broken, she will lick her vulva to clean herself and labor is quick to follow.

Puppies are covered in a thick, slippery membrane when they are born. This is usually licked away by the mother, and the umbilical cord is severed by her chewing. The puppy cannot breathe until the membrane is removed, so if the mother fails to do this, act quickly, by breaking the membrane with your fingers. The umbilical cord needs to be tied close to the puppy's abdomen and the cord cut with a pair of clean, sharp scissors about an inch (2.5 cm) away, between the thread and the placenta.

Generally, domestic dogs give birth without problem. As each puppy is born, it should be given a chance to suckle, which helps to stimulate the

contractions for the next one. Once all the puppies are born, the mother will be tired and will need to relieve herself. Offer her a drink, then let her relax with her new family.

It normally takes around six hours for a large litter to be born. There may be a problem if a bitch strains for more than two hours to produce one pup, or if she continues to strain after all the pups appear to have been born. Veterinary help should then be sought immediately.

the new puppies
The new arrivals are completely

above: *Exploration starts at around 3–4 weeks. Puppies become more mobile and independent at this time.*

dependent on their mother. Born blind and deaf and without the ability to walk or even urinate or defecate without their mother's licking to stimulate them, they have much development ahead of them. Part of this development is to become familiar with people—their smell and touch, so it is important that you handle the puppies from day one. Socialization cannot start too early—each and every one of these puppies will depend on you for the best possible start in life.

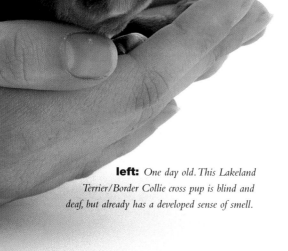

left: *One day old. This Lakeland Terrier/Border Collie cross pup is blind and deaf, but already has a developed sense of smell.*

below: *Six weeks old and six years old. Puppies develop at an incredible rate!*

What to do if your bitch is mated accidentally

Many unwanted puppies are born each year because dogs and bitches can be quite determined to mate, even where their owners are careful and vigilant. Veterinary intervention, in the form of an injection or tablets, can end the pregnancy as long as the bitch is taken to a clinic as soon as possible. Such intervention is not common practice in the United States, due to potential side effects.

Three's a crowd!

Even though a bitch has already been mated to one dog during her fertile period, it is perfectly possible for her to mate another a few days later and conceive on both occasions. Such litters may be a real mixture of pups—some resembling one father and some the other!

competing and working with dogs

Dogs have become much more to man than simple working partners. Humans are a competitive race, and dogs have been used to compete in various sports for many hundreds of years.

The earliest of these sports are recognized as cruel and distasteful to us now. Bear baiting, dog fighting, and ratting were all considered a fair test of

below: *A Basenji being examined by a judge. She checks for soundness and conformation according to the breed standard.*

a dog's strength, where the owner could place a bet on his dog being the ultimate victor. Of course, such abuse is now illegal, and other dog sports have taken over.

dog racing

Racing is probably the most common of these. Greyhounds are the best known competitors at this sport—bred and trained to chase an electric hare around a track, these dogs can reach incredible speeds, and thoroughly

enjoy the job for which they were bred. Sadly, their racing life is usually short, and this means that many ex-racers are looking for new homes, making them one of the most common breeds in animal shelters.

Other breeds are also raced from time to time. Terrier racing is fast and furious, while Afghan Hound racing allows these dogs to pursue their original career in the most elegant way—with their long coats flowing out behind them as they sail around the track.

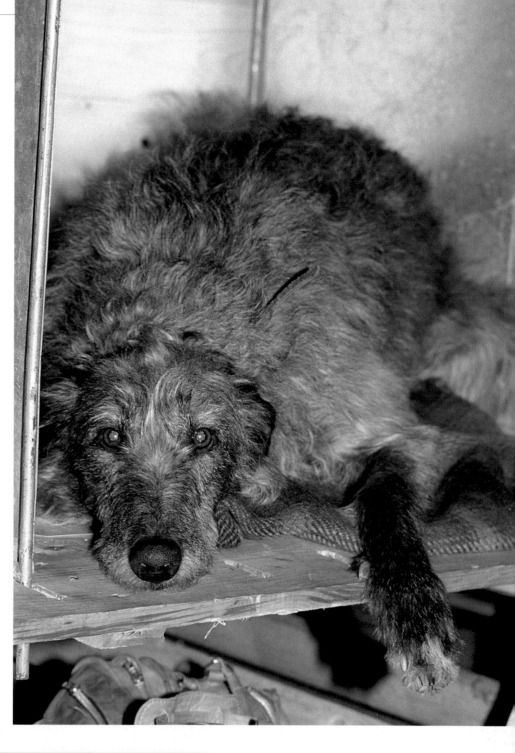

right: *A Deerhound rests on his bench at a championship show—it's been a long day!*

sheepdog trials

Collies and other herders have always been used as working dogs to round up sheep and cattle and bring them off a hillside. However, even shepherds cannot resist a wager, and the sport of sheepdog trialing began. In these contests, dogs are required to follow a set pattern of herding and penning. These trials require great skill and precision from both the trainer and the dog.

field trials

Gundog tests and field trials also give trainers a chance to compete in a sport for which their dogs were bred. All the retrievers and spaniels are well represented at such events where the dogs are required to show their ability to locate and pick up game, as well as bring it back, unmarked, to the handler. Such trials are usually set in wonderful countryside and dogs are often worked through water at great distances.

working trials

Working trials are designed to test a dog in several different areas—control work, tracking, finding hidden objects, and agility. Some areas of this sport

also require the dog to be able to find and hold a "criminal"—either by keeping him in one spot by barking or by holding him by the arm.

agility

Agility is now a highly popular sport in many countries. A little like show jumping for dogs, the dog is trained to maneuver a number of different obstacles—through tunnels, over jumps, and along narrow walkways and seesaws. The dog must complete the

left: *Specially trained, some working dogs can provide protection for their handlers.*

course in a set order without refusing any obstacle or incurring any "faults" in the fastest time. All breeds are used to compete in agility, but the speed of the Collies is usually unmatched.

obedience competition

These tests are designed to show how accurately a dog has been trained to follow a set pattern of formal exercises. Close heelwork, sits, downs, retrieves,

below: *A military display showing working dogs on parade.*

and "send aways" are all included and are marked by the judge. The fewer marks lost, the better the performance.

flyball

Flyball is a relatively new sport—but is great fun! Dogs are usually run in teams with one member from each team racing the other in a relay. Each dog has to leap over several small jumps before reaching a box that contains a ball. The dogs are trained to step on a pedal on the box so that the ball comes flying out. The dog must

then return over the same route with the ball before the next dog can go.

dancing with dogs

New dog sports are being thought up all the time. "Freestyle dancing with dogs" was originally based on obedience heelwork set to music, but has since incorporated tricks, such as the dog weaving in and out of the handler's legs, spinning, or walking backward—all in time to the beat. The music is usually "themed" to make this a real spectacle for the dog, handler,

and spectators alike.

As a result of this exciting new sport, other, more basic forms of dancing with dogs have taken off. Line dancing with dogs is now popular as a way of training dogs in basic obedience while enjoying a day out, too!

beauty shows

Breed shows are all about competing to find the dog that most closely resembles its own breed "standard." The breed standards are laid down by the national kennel clubs and highlight the way the dog looks, moves, and, to a certain extent, behaves.

Dog shows vary in formality from a Sunday afternoon in the local park to a championship show at the highest level, such as the Westminster Show.

Most dogs are "schooled" before entering a dog show. They are expected to stand still for the judge's examination and trot at a set pace when asked to move. Winning dogs are likely to receive rosettes and can compete to become champions if they gain a sufficient number of prizes.

dogs in service

Dogs have given far more to man than simple companionship. Over the centuries, dogs have been used as camp cleaners, hunting partners, and alarm raisers, but these days, the tasks we ask of dogs are even more sophisticated. Guide dogs for the blind were first trained in Germany after the end of the First World War, for soldiers who had come home visually disabled. A full training scheme was devised and put into action in Britain in 1930, with other countries soon following suit. It wasn't long before dogs were being used to assist people with other disabilities. Programs like Dogs for the Disabled and Support Dogs proved that dogs could do a lot more than just act as a guide. Trained dogs are able to pick up dropped items, take money into stores, and even load and unload the

washing machine!

Detection work—such as sniffing out illegal drugs—is also well known, and dogs have now been trained to search for other items, too, such as

left: More than just a friend, a service dog handler may depend on his canine partner to save his life.

illegally imported fruit and vegetables, and even dry rot. Search and rescue dogs are trained to find those lost on snow-covered hillsides, or in urban searches in towns and cities. Dogs have even been used to find the bodies of people who have died in disasters.

More recently, dogs have also begun to show potential in other work. Dogs that can detect cancers before they develop, and those that can predict the onset of epileptic seizures in their human owners, are proving that dogs not only enhance our lives—they can save them, too.

below: Some dogs give more than just companionship. "Assistance dogs" offer their disabled owners a lifeline.

the glossary

Albino A dog with a white or ivory coat and pink or blue eyes, caused by a defective gene that inhibits pigment formation.

Bat ear A type of ear that is rounded with a broad base, as in Bulldogs.

Bird dog A breed developed to hunt game birds.

Bite The relative alignment of the upper and lower sets of teeth when the mouth is closed.

Blanket A solid coat color that extends from the neck to the tail along the back and upper part of the sides.

Blaze A central white stripe along the face, usually running between the eyes.

Blocky head A squarish head, as in the Boston Terrier.

Blue-black Hair with a blue base and black tip.

Bobtail An alternative term for the Old English Sheepdog, or for a dog that naturally lacks a tail or has one docked very short.

Button ear A folded-down ear that lies close to the head so that it covers the ear opening.

Clip A styled coat cut, such as the "lion cut" in Poodles.

Coat The hair covering a dog; may be either single or double.

Collar Markings, usually white, found around the neck.

Companion dog A canine that has earned a specified score in obedience trials at a number of kennel club-licensed events, and has consequently been awarded the "CD" suffix to be used with the dog's name.

Cream A light yellow coat.

Cropping A method (cutting or trimming) for inducing the ears to stand erect; not permitted in some countries.

Culottes Longer hair on the back of the thighs that give a dog a "baggy trousers" look, such as in the Schipperke.

Curled tail A tightly curled (single or double) tail held close to the back or buttocks, although the tip may be held high.

Dish-faced A foreface (from the stop to the nose tip) that forms a slightly concave profile, as in the Pointer.

Dock To amputate the greater part of the tail to make it short.

Dog show A sanctioned championship competition that may be for all breeds or for a single breed (the latter is called a specialty show).

Double coat A coat that has both an outer layer of hair resistant to weather and an inner layer of softer hair for warmth and waterproofing.

Down-faced A muzzle that inclines downward from the top of the skull to the tip of the nose, as in the Bull Terrier.

Drop ear An ear that is folded forward partly or completely over the ear opening.

Ear guide dog A canine that is specially trained to guide the deaf.

Even bite The condition in which the front teeth (upper and lower incisors) meet with no overlap when the mouth is closed.

Feathering Patches of longer hairs on the ends of the ears, legs, tail, or body.

Full coat A coat that has attained mature length.

Guard hairs Generally stiff hairs that are longer and smoother than those of the undercoat through which they grow, and which they conceal.

Gundog A specially trained dog or breed able to work with its master in finding and retrieving live or shot game.

Handler The person controlling a dog in the show ring or field trial; if receiving a fee for this service, this person is called a professional handler.

Hand-pluck To pluck an undercoat with fingertips.

Harlequin A coat pattern of usually black or blue patches on a white ground as is found in Great Danes.

Haw A third eyelid (or nictitating membrane) found in the inside corner of the eye in some breeds.

Height Sometimes referred to as shoulder height, this vertical measurement is taken from the withers to the ground.

Hock Essentially the dog's true heel, composed of the tarsus, or the collection of bones of the hind leg forming the joint between the lower thigh and the metatarsus.

Hook tail A tail that is carried down, but with the tip curled upward.

Hound A dog developed for hunting by scent or sight.

Hound-marked A coat coloration composed of tan and/or black patches usually on the head, back, legs, and tail, on a generally white ground.

Hunting dog A grouping that includes both gundogs that hunt game and hounds that hunt other animals.

Kink tail A bent tail caused by a malformation of the caudal vertebrae.

Lead A leash attached to a collar or harness for restraining or leading a dog.

Level bite The condition in which the front teeth (upper and lower incisors) meet exactly edge-to-edge with no overlap when the mouth is closed.

Mane An abundance of long hair found on the nape and sides of the neck.

Marking A small patch of contrasting-colored hairs, usually on the head or body.

Mask A foreface that is darkly shaded such as in the Mastiff, Boxer, and Pekingese.

Mat A rather firm corded coat such as is found in the Puli and Komondor.

Muzzle The foreface, consisting of the nasal bone, nostrils, jaws, and head in front of the eyes.

Neoteny The retention of juvenile characteristics in adulthood, for example, barking in dogs.

Nose bridge The straight or arched upper side of the muzzle from the stop to the nose.

Pad A tough, thickened skin projection on the underside of the feet that serves as a shock absorber.

Pedigree A recorded, usually written, description of at least three generations of a dog's ancestry.

Pied A coat composed of relatively large unequally proportioned patches of two or more colors, one usually being white.

Pluck To remove hairs from the overcoat using either one's fingertips or a stripper.

Plume As the name implies, a long fringe of hair that hangs from the tail.

Point The stance taken by a hunting dog (hound or gundog) when it stands still to indicate the presence and position of game.

Point of hock The outer angle of the hock.

Point of shoulder The joint on the body where the upper leg meets the scapula.

Points Small patches of a contrasting color, usually white, black, or tan, on the face, ears, legs, and tail.

Prick ear A usually pointed ear, carried fully erect.

Pup Officially a dog less than one year old.

Puppy clip A cut style used for Poodles of nine to 12 months old, in which the hairs on the face, feet, and tail root are clipped, leaving the long hairs elsewhere.

Rat tail A tapered tail that is thick at the root, and partially or completely devoid of hair, such as in the Irish Water Spaniel.

Register A record filed with the national kennel club of a dog's breeding particulars.

Ring tail An almost fully circular tail that is carried up.

Roman nose A nose with a bridge so comparatively high as to form a slightly convex line from the forehead to the nose tip.

Rose ear A small drop ear, as seen in Bulldogs, that folds over and back.

Ruff A growth of longer, thicker hair around the neck.

Rough coat A usually medium-to-long coarse overcoat.

Sable An inherited coat color of black-tipped hairs on a basically silver, gray, gold, fawn, or brown ground.

Saddle A black marking shaped and placed as named.

Socks Slightly longer hair on a dog's feet up to the pasterns and/or dewclaws.

Solid or self color A coat completely of one color.

Spectacles As the name implies, a shading or dark marking, shaped and situated like eyeglasses.

Spotted Coin-sized black or liver patches sprinkled all over a white body, such as in the Dalmatian.

Squirrel tail A curved tail that is carried up and forward.

Stop The point at which the nasal bones and cranium meet, marked by a step up from the muzzle to the skull or an indentation between the eyes.

Ticked A white coat sparsely covered with small patches of black, flecked, or colored hairs.

Tricolor A coat of three distinct colors, usually white, black, and tan.

Trim To groom a dog's coat by plucking or clipping.

Tulip ear A rather wide ear carried erect and somewhat forward with the edges curving slightly inward.

Turn-up An upturned foreface or underjaw, such as in the Bulldog.

Undercoat A dense, soft, short coat concealed by a longer topcoat.

Walleye Also known as fisheye, glass eye, or pearl eye, this type of eye has a pale bluish, whitish, or colorless iris.

Wire-haired A harsh, crisp, wiry textured coat that serves as protection against bad weather and enemies.

Withers The point just behind the neck from which the dog's body height is measured.

index